BRUNSWICK COUNTY [VIRGINIA] ROAD ORDERS

1732-1746

Virginia Genealogical Society
Richmond, Virginia

Published With Permission from the

Virginia Transportation Research Council
(A Cooperative Organization Sponsored Jointly by the Virginia
Department of Transportation and
the University of Virginia)

HERITAGE BOOKS
2008

HERITAGE BOOKS
AN IMPRINT OF HERITAGE BOOKS, INC.

Books, CDs, and more—Worldwide

For our listing of thousands of titles see our website
at
www.HeritageBooks.com

Published 2008 by
HERITAGE BOOKS, INC.
Publishing Division
100 Railroad Avenue #104
Westminster, Maryland 21157

Copyright © 1988, 2004 Virginia Genealogical Society

All rights reserved. No part of this book may be reproduced or transmitted in any form or by any means, electronic or mechanical, including photocopying, recording or by any information storage and retrieval system without written permission from the author, except for the inclusion of brief quotations in a review.

International Standard Book Number: 978-0-7884-3660-4

BRUNSWICK COUNTY ROAD ORDERS 1732-1746
By
Nathaniel Mason Pawlett
Faculty Research Historian

(The opinions, findings, and conclusions expressed in this
report are those of the author and not necessarily those of
the sponsoring agencies.)

Virginia Transportation Research Council
(A Cooperative Organization Sponsored Jointly by the Virginia
Department of Transportation and
the University of Virginia)

Charlottesville, Virginia

July 1988
Revised May 2004
VTRC 89-R1

Historic Roads of Virginia

Louisa County Road Orders 1742-1748, by Nathaniel Mason Pawlett. 57 pages, indexed, map.

Goochland County Road Orders 1728-1744, by Nathaniel Mason Pawlett. 120 pages, indexed, map.

Albemarle County Road Orders 1744-1748, by Nathaniel Mason Pawlett. 52 pages, indexed, map.

The Route of the Three Notch'd Road, by Nathaniel Mason Pawlett and Howard Newlon, Jr. 26 pages, illustrated, 2 maps.

An Index to Roads in the Albemarle County Surveyors Books 1744-1853, by Nathaniel Mason Pawlett. 10 pages, map.

A Brief History of the Staunton and James River Turnpike, by Douglas Young, 22 pages, illustrated, map.

Albemarle County Road Orders 1783-1816, by Nathaniel Mason Pawlett. 421 pages, indexed.

A Brief History of the Roads of Virginia 1607-1840, by Nathaniel Mason Pawlett. 41 pages, 3 maps.

A Guide to the Preparation of County Road Histories, by Nathaniel Mason Pawlett. 26 pages, 2 maps.

Early Road Location: Key to Discovering Historic Resources? by Nathaniel Mason Pawlett and K. Edward Lay. 47 pages, illustrated, 3 maps.

Albemarle County Roads 1725-1816, by Nathaniel Mason Pawlett. 98 pages, illustrated, 5 maps.

Backsights: A Bibliography, by Nathaniel Mason Pawlett. 29 pages.

Orange County Road Orders 1734-1749, by Ann Brush Miller. 323 pages, indexed, map.

Spotsylvania County Road Orders 1722-1734, by Nathaniel Mason Pawlett. 152 pages, indexed, map.

A Note on the Methods, Editing and Dating System

The road and bridge orders contained in the order books of an early Virginia county are the primary source of information for the study of its roads. When extracted, indexed and published by the Virginia Transportation Research Council, they greatly facilitate this. All of the early county court order books are in manuscript, sometimes so damaged and faded as to be almost indecipherable. Usually rendered in the rather ornate copperplate script of the time, the phonetic spellings of this period often serve to further complicate matters for the researcher and recorder.

The amount of material to be handled, as well as the number of people involved, renders virtually useless the idea of longhand transcription. This same problem had been faced at the beginning of the Albemarle road study some years before, although the difficult nature of the Louisa records had initially forced the author to resort to longhand transcription for them. Shortly, however, in order to facilitate the work, a system was devised to render these road orders literatim into a small hand-held tape recorder and reproduce for transcription all their eighteenth-century idiosyncrasies. This recording system might be set out in the following rather general rules:

1. Capitalisation to be so stated. Viz: "cap Wadlow cap Cuthbert cap Twaddle" in the case of the name Wadlow Cuthbert Twaddle and any other words in the road order which are capitalised.

2. Names with variant or phonetic spellings to be spelled out. Do not assume that the common Virginian spelling is the only one.

3. No periods unless so stated.

4. Periods, commas, colons, semicolons, etc., to be stated. All symbols to be described as nearly as possible.

5. Date and pagination in order book, vestry book, etc., to be stated. Pre-1752 dates to be designated O.S. for Old Style.

6. Each new citation to be so stated.

7. No paragraphing unless so stated.

8. Tape reels to be marked sequentially as completed, with county, name of record, book number(s), and approximate date covered.

Following this, the orders were put into typescript by a secretary who had to unlearn many of the modern rules of spelling and then learn to render the orders exactly as dictated. Then the transcripts were compared to the tapes or to the original manuscript sources and corrected. Placed in their final form and indexed, the road orders were ready for publication and distribution.

With these road orders available in an indexed and cross-referenced published form, it will be possible to produce chronological chains of road orders illustrating the development of many of the early roads of a vast area from the threshold of settlement up through the middle of the eighteenth century. Immediate corroboration for these chains of early road orders will usually be provided by other evidence such as deeds, plats and the Confederate Engineers maps. Often, in fact, the principal roads will be found to survive in place under their early names.

With regard to the general editorial principles of the project, it has been our perception over the years as the road orders of Louisa, Hanover, Goochland and Albemarle have been examined and recorded that road orders themselves are really a variety of "notes", often cryptic, incomplete or based on assumptions concerning the level of knowledge of the reader. As such, any further abstracting or compression of them would tend to produce "notes" taken from "notes", making them even less comprehensible. The tendency has therefore been in the direction of restraint in editing, leaving any conclusions with regard to meaning up to the individual reader or researcher using these publications. In pursuing this course we have attempted to present the reader with a typescript text which is as near a type facsimile of the manuscript itself as we can come.

Our objective is to produce a text that conveys as near the precise form of the original as we can, reproducing all the peculiarities of the eighteenth century orthography. While some compromises have had to be made due to the keyboard of the modern typewriter, this was really not that difficult a task. Most of their symbols can be accommodated by modern typography, and most abbreviations are fairly clear as to meaning.

Punctuation may appear misleading at times, with unnecessary commas or commas placed where periods should be located; appropriate terminal punctuation is often missing or else takes the form of a symbol such as a long dash, etc. The original capitalisation has been retained insofar as it was possible to determine from the original manuscript whether capitals were intended. No capitals have been inserted in place of those originally omitted. The original spelling and syntax have been retained throughout, even including the obvious errors in various places, such as repetitions of words and simple clerical errors. Ampersands have been retained throughout to include such forms as "&c.ª" for "etc." Superscript letters have also been retained where used in yᵉ., yᵗ., sᵈ. The thorn symbol (y), pronounced as "th," has been retained in the aforesaid "yᵉ.", pronounced "the", and "yᵗ." (that), along with the tailed p (ℒ) which the limitations of the modern typewriter have forced us to render as a capital "p". This should be taken to mean either "per" (by), "pre" or "pro" (sometimes "par" as in "Pish" for parish) as the context by the order may demand. For damaged and missing portions of the manuscript we have used square brackets to denote the [missing], [torn] or [illegible] portions. Due to the large number of ancient forms of spelling, grammar and syntax it has been deemed impracticable to insert the form [sic] after each one to indicate a literal rendering. Therefore, the reader must assume that apparent errors are merely the result of our literal transcription of the road orders, barring the introduction of typographical errors of course. If in any case this appears to present insuperable problems, resort should be made to the original records available for examination at Brunswick Court House.

As to dating, most historians and genealogists who have worked with early Virginian records will be aware of the English dating system in use down to 1752. Although there was an eleven-day difference from our calendar in the day of the month, the principal difference lay in the fact that the beginning of the year was dated from March 25 rather than January 1, as was the case from 1752 onward to the present. Thus January, February and March (to the 25th) were the last three months in a given year and the new year came in only on March 25.

Early Virginian records usually follow this practice, though in some cases dates during these three months will be shown in the form 1732/3, showing both the English date and that in use on the Continent, where the year began January 1. For researchers using material with dates in the English style it is important to remember that under this system (for instance) a man might die in January 1734 yet convey property or serve in public office in June 1734, since June came before January in a given year under this system.

BRUNSWICK COUNTY ROAD ORDERS 1732-1746

By

Nathaniel Mason Pawlett
Faculty Research Historian

INTRODUCTION

> The roads are under the government of the county courts, subject to be controuled by the general court. They order new roads to be opened whenever they think them necessary. The inhabitants of the county are by them laid off into precincts, to each of which they allot a convenient portion of the public roads to be kept in repair. Such bridges as may be built without the assistance of artificers, they are to be built. If the stream be such as to require a bridge of regular workmanship, the court employs workmen to build it, at the expense of the whole county. If it be too great for the county, application is made to the general assembly, who authorize individuals to build it, and to take a fixed toll from all passengers, or give sanction to such other proposition as to them appears reasonable.
>
> Thomas Jefferson, *Notes on the State of Virginia, 1781*.

The establishment and maintenance of public roads was one of the most important functions of the County Court during the colonial period in Virginia. Each road was opened and maintained by an Overseer of Highways appointed by the Gentlemen Justices yearly. He was usually assigned all the "Labouring Male Titheables" living on or near the road for this purpose. These individuals then furnished all their own tools, wagons, and teams and were required to labour for six days each year on the roads.

Major projects, such as bridges over rivers, demanding considerable expenditures were executed by Commissioners appointed by the Court to select the site and to contract with workmen for the construction. Where bridges connected two counties, a commission was appointed by each and they cooperated in executing the work.

At its inception, Brunswick County comprised a large part of the Piedmont frontier east of the Blue Ridge and south of the James River, the as yet unsettled lands stretching westward to the Blue Ridge. Its distant boundary was intended both to facilitate western settlement and to increase the county's effectiveness as a buffer against the French influence advancing into the center of the continent.

From 1732 to 1746 Brunswick was a giant parent county; by the end of this time, it had shrunk to very nearly its present size. The scale of the county as originally conceived made administration unwieldy, and like other large frontier counties created as a response to continued westward movement. Brunswick lost the majority of its territoroty within about twenty-five years of its creation.

The road orders contained in this volume cover the period from 1732, when Brunswick's county government first became operational, through the creation of Lunenburg County in 1746. As such they are the principal extant evidence concerning the early development of a vast area of Southside Virginia stretching as far as the Blue Ridge.

THE DEVELOPMENT OF BRUNSWICK COUNTY

Note: As originally published in paper format, this volume included maps showing the evolution of the county. Maps are not included in the revised/electronic version due to legibility and file size considerations. Instead, a verbal description is provided.

As originally formed (created in 1720, and with its county government established in 1732), Brunswick County was a giant county, covering a large portion of Southside Virginia. Its boundaries extended eastward as far as modern Southampton, westward to the Blue Ridge Mountains, southward to North Carolina, and northward to Botetourt County. Within its borders were the modern counties of Greensville, Brunswick, Lunenburg, Mecklenburg, Charlotte, Halifax, Pittsylvania, Henry, Patrick and Franklin, as well as portions of Bedford, Campbell, and Appomattox counties.

With the creation of Lunenburg County in 1746, Brunswick was reduced to a fraction of its former size, comprising only modern day Brunswick and Greensville counties. The creation of Greensville County in 1781 left Brunswick at its present boundaries.

Brunswick County Order Book 1

1 June 1732 Old Style, Page 3
John Rose is apointed Surveyor of the Road from Reedy Creek to this Court House And it is Ordered that he with the Male Labouring Tithable persons belonging to Joseph Warberton. John Evans, James Arnold James ann William Duke John Edwards James Duke and John Duke the same --

1 June 1732 Old Style, Page 4
Charles Kimball is apointed Surveyor of the High Way [missing in book] County Line to the Reedy Creek in this County And It is ordered [missing in book] with the Male Labouring Tithable persons belonging to Ralph [missing] Thomas Jackson Edward Tatum Joseph Kimbal Joseph [missing] John Seering William Gower Richard Huckabee John Harwell William Pool Robert Dier Robert Renard John Cook and Charles Kimball [missing] the same according to Law --

1 June 1732 Old Style, Page 4
Robert Humphries is apointed to clear a Road from Nottoway River to the Chappel in this County And it is Ordered that he with all the Male Labouring Tithable persons belonging to Richard Smith Richard Swansomes & Saml Crawley clear the same according to Law --

6 July 1732 Old Style, Page 5
William Smith is apointed Surveyor of the High Waies from the Mouth of Haw Tree on the South side of Roenoke River up to the first great Creek And it is Ordered that he with the Tithable persons convenient thereto clear & repair the same --

6 July 1732 Old Style, Page 5
William Hagood is apointed Surveyor of the High Waies from Maherrin River to the Church And 'tis Ordered that the Tithable persons that were in Bedin [missing] Order on this side the River Assist him in clearing the same --

6 July 1732 Old Style, Page 5
Thomas Wilson is apointed Surveyor of the High Waies from the Horse fford over Roenoke River to the Ridge between Roenoke and Maherrin River And that all the Male Labouring Tithables below Stith's Creek assist him in clearing the same --

6 July 1732 O. S., Page 5
Henry Bedingfield is apointed Surveyor of the High Waies from the upper Cut Banks on Maherrin River to the Main Ridge between Maherrin & Roanoke Rivers And it is Ordered that all the Male Labouring Tithable persons between Taylors Creek and the fort Assist him in clearing the same --

6 July 1732 O. S., Page 5
John Butcher is apointed Surveyor of the High Waies from Munford's Quarter up Roenoke the most convenient way into Wilsons and Bedingfield's Road And it is Ordered that he with all the Male Labouring Tithable persons above Stiths Creek clear the same --

3 August 1732 O. S., Page 8
Samuel fflowers is appointed Surveyor of the High Waies from Nottoway River near Richard Burkes to Sturgeon Run And it is Ordered that the Tithable persons in Capt Embry's order Assist him in clearing the same

3 August 1732 O. S., Page 8
William Macklin gent is apointed Surveyor of the High Waies from Maherrin River above his Own House And it is Ordered that all the Male Labouring Tithables from Coll^o Harrisons Quarters and upwards Assist him in clearing the same --

3 August 1732 O. S., Page 8
Henry Hoe Henry Embry and George Walton gent or any two of them are apointed and desired to treat with the Court of Prince George County about the Building of such Bridge or Bridges over Nottoway River And at such place or places as they and the Gent apointed by Prince George County shall agree And that they also agree with any Workman to [missing] Building thereof --

2 November 1732 0. S., Page 14
Robert Humphries is apointed Surveyor of the High Waies from Rockey Creek to Jones ffoard in the Room of William Jones And it is Ordered that all the Male Labouring Tithable persons above Hickory Run Asist him in clearing the same --

2 November 1732 O. S., Page 14
Edward Tatum is apointed Surveyor of the High Waies from the Reedy Creek below Jacksons Mill the nearest Way to the Church And it is Ordered that all the Male Labouring Tithable persons assist him in clearing the same which are on the Rocky & Reedy Creeks.

1 February 1732 O. S., Page 16
On the Consideration of the petition of William Wall to be added to the tyths on the upper Road it is ordered that the Same be thrown out --

1 February 1732 O. S., Page 16
Henry Morris is appointed to Clear a briddle Road from Jerimiah Mizes to Munfords Quarter up Roanoke and it is ordered that he and all the Male Labouring Tyhable persons above Butchers Creek assist in Clearing the Same --

1 February 1732 O. S., Page 16
John Butcher is appointed Surveyor of the high Way from a ford on Roanoke a little below Butchers into Bedingfields Road and that all the male Labouring Tyths between Stith's and Butchers Creek and all above Cotton Creek on the South Side of Roanoake River assist in Clearing the Same --

1 February 1732 O. S., Page 16
Samuel Chamberlain is appointed Surveyor of the Road from the west ward path down to Doctor Irby's and that all the Tythables in the old order assist in Clearing the Same --

1 March 1732 O. S., Page 18
Henry ffox John Wall and George Walton or any two of them are appointed and desired to treat with the Court of Prince George County about the building of a Bridge over Nottoway River at or near the Lower cut hanks as they and the Gentlemen Apointed by Prince George Court Shall agree and that they also agree with Some person or persons to undertake the building thereof --

1 March 1732 O. S., Page 18
Charles Kimball and John Ross are ordered to Assist Edward Tatum and his Gang in Clearing a briddle way from the Ready Creek below Jackson's Mill the most Convenient Way in to the Road that Leads from this Courthouse to Surry County --

5 April 1733 O. S., Page 22
Henry ffox John Wall and Geo: Wallton Gent. or any two of them are appointed and desired to treat with the Gent. of the Court of Prince George County at such time as they think most convenient that they appoint some of their Members to meet them in order to treat with persons to undertake the building of a bridge over Nottoway River at or near the Lower cut banks --

6 April 1733 O. S., Page 24
Henry Wych is Appointed Surveyor of the high Way from Hick's Ford to the County Line and the hands that usually cleard it assist him in Repairing the Same --

6 April 1773 O. S., Page 24
John Wall Gent is appointed Surveyor of a Briddle Road from his Mill to Chamberlains Ford and that the Tyths of Henry Fox John Irby John Chapman George Brewer, William Linch, Joseph Heathrock and his own assist in Clearing the Same –

6 April 1733 O. S., Page 24
Marmaduke Johnson is Appointed Surveyor of the High Way from Chunketapusso to Bedingfield's Road and that all the male Labouring Tyths between Coldwater Run and the Great Creek assist in Clearing the Same --

6 April 1733 O. S., Page 24
John Douglass is Appointed Surveyor of a Briddle Way from Chamberlain's ford to Jackson's Mill Swamp were Tatum's Road Crosses it and that all the Male Laboring tyths belonging to Samuel Chamberlain Richard Weatherford Col^l Allen Mary Syms John Jackson John Leadbetter David bails James and Lizwell Saxon [?] Assist With their own hands in Clearing the Same --

7 June 1733 O. S., Page 26
Henry Cook is appointed Surveyor of a Road from Capp^t Poytris's Plantation on ffountain's Creek to Henry Wych's fford over Meherrin and [missing] all the Male Labouring Tyths between the Cane branch and the G[missing] Swamp and that James Parham, John Clyburn, John Walker, Thomas Busbey, Thomas Burnett & ffrancis Steed assist in Clearing the Same --

7 June 1733 O. S., Page 28
Henry Embry William Wynne and Charles King Gent. or any two of them are Impower'd and Required to treat with the Court of Prince George that they appoint Some of their Members to meet them in order to agree with Some person to undertake the building of Such bridge or Bridges over Nottoway River and at Such place or places as they Can agree on --

5 July 1733 O. S., Page 29
Ordered that the Road from Douglass's Wolf Pit to Adam Sim's ford be Reduced to a briddle Way only --

2 August 1733 O. S., Page 32
A Supersedeas being obtained against an order of this Court Granted the Seventh of June Last for building a bridge over Nottoway River which being Executed and Notice thereof Given to the Court Henry ffox & John Wall Gent. are appointed to attend the Generall Court to Maintain the Supersedeas --

6 September 1733 O. S., Page 33
Henry Bedingfield is appointd overseer of the High way from the Ridge between Roanoake and Meherrin, to Maherrin River and from the fort to the other Road above where Carghill lived and that all the Tyths in Marmaduke Johnson's Order Assist in Clearing the Same and also those in his own former order --

6 September 1733 O. S., Page 33
William Vaughan is appointed overseer of a Road from the old Brunswick Line to Sweeds ford on Nottoway and that all Tyths in the former order Except Hosea Tapley John Jackson, William Whittamore and William Smith assist in Clearing the Same --

6 September 1733 O. S., Page 33
Hosea Tapley is Appointed overseer of the Road from the old Brunswick Line to the Reedy Creek and that all the Tyths between Honey Hill run the old County Line and the three Creeks assist also Hosea Tapley John Jackson William Whittamore and William Smith assist in Clearing the Same.

6 September 1733 O. S., Page 34
William Maclin Gent is Appointed Surveyor of a Church Road from Harrison's Quarter on the Great Creek to the Church and that all the Tyths in his former order assist in Clearing the Same --

6 September 1733 O. S., Page 35
Thomas Wilson is ordered with his Gang to Assist Henry bedingfield and his Gang to Clear the Road from the fort to the Roanoake Road and that John Ezell and William Sinkfield be added to the Said Bedingfield's order --

4 October 1733 O. S., Page 36
ffrancis Wyrick is appointed Surveyor of a Road from the County Lyne by Thomas Jordan's to Nathaniel Perry's and that all the Male Labouring Tyths belonging to Thomas Parsons, James Haley, John ffennell, Robert Hill Joseph Parks, William Parks Lewis Dupre', John Lucas, Benjamin Wray Edward Wearham, Simon Turner, and Michael Sullivant with all on the South Side of ffountains Creek assist in Clearing the Same --

4 October 1733 O. S., Page 36
Matthew Parham is appointed to Clear the Road from opposite to Nathaniel Perry's into Henry Cooks Road Near Michael Wall's Plantation where the Widdow trap lives and that all the Male Labouring Tyths belonging to Charles Jenkins, Thomas Hewit William Smith, William Smith ju^r Batte Petterson Gent. M^r. Battes Quarter Thomas Reaves, James Lunday, Nathaniel Perry Timothy Reaves William Cate, Burwell Brown, Edmond ^{m}.Carty Thomas Carter Thomas Reaves ju^r Jeremiah Brown, Robert Douglass, William Douglass, ffoster Reaves, & Robert Hicks assist him and his Tyths in Clearing the Same --

4 October 1733 O. S., Page 37
Thomas Jackson is appointed Surveyor of a Road from Chamberlains fford the Convenientest Way into the Old Road at the Little Creek bridge thence along the old Road untill it is Convenient to turn Round Coll Allens Plantation between Allens and Howses and that all the male Labouring Tyths belonging to John Jackson, David Bailes, John Ledbetter, James Watson, Ambros Jackson, Samuel Harwell Samuel Kyrk, William Sims, John Tomerlin, William Collier Laurance Higgins, Thomas Venton, and Coll Allens Quarter Assist in clearing the Same

4 October 1733 O. S., Page 37
John Davis is Appointed Surveyor of the high Way from Thomas Houses to Harrison's Quarter Called Sweeds and that all Male Labouring Tyths to Thomas House Thomas House ju^r James House Willm. House, Wil^m. Wrenn Henry Bates, Joseph Wrenn assist in Clearing the Same --

4 October 1733 O. S., Page 38
John Davis is appointed Overseer of the High Way in Stead of Willm Smith over Roanoake and that all the Tyths in the Said Smith's order assist in Clearing the Same --

4 October 1733 O. S., Page 38
A Supersedeas being obtain'd by Henry ffox and others against an order of this Court Granted the Seventh of June Last for building a bridge over Nottoway River and the Same being Executed and Notice thereof Given to the Court Henry ffox and John Wall Gent. are appointed to attend the Generall Court to Maintain the aforesaid Supersedeas --

6 October 1733 O. S., Page 42
Ordered that a Road be Cleared from Robert Humpris's into Burch's Road along the Ridge between Sturgeon Run and Waqua and that John Wyrick William Reaves, Mason Bishop Samuel Crawley John Meritt and James Rigsby Assist Clem^t. Read and his people in Clearing the Same --

7 February 1733 O. S., Page 53
Henry Embry John Wall and John Duke or any two of them are appointed and desired to treat with the Court of Surry County that they appoint some of there members to meet them in order to agree about building a bridge over Nottoway River at Such Place as they can agree --

7 February 1733 O. S., Page 53
It is ordered that William and Charles Dodson be added to John Wall and that John Wall is appointed Overseer instead of Samuel Flowers --

7 February 1733 O. S., Page 53
John Naper Petitioning this Court it is ordered that he be Exempted from Clearing the High Way

7 February 1733 O. S., Page 53
Robert Humphris is appointed Surveyor of a Road from Nottoway River to Waqua and it is ordered that all the tyths above Richard Smith's between Nottoway and Waqua Assist in Clearing the Same --

7 February 1733 O. S., Page 53
Clement Read is Appointed Surveyor of a Road from Waqua into the Church Road and it is ordered that Richard Ramsey Mason Bishop William Douglass

Samuel Crawley, William Reaves, John Meritt, Josias Randle & Rigsbey With their tyths assist in Clearing the Same --

7 February 1733 O. S., Page 53
It is ordered that William Walters & Joseph Dunman with their tyths be added to Maclins Order

7 March 1733 O. S., Page 56
Upon the Petition of Roger Tillman and the Court Considering on the matter it is thereupon ordered that he have leave to build a bridge over Nottoway River Att the Most Convenient place between the Mouth of Sturgeon Run and the Lower cutt banks --

7 March 1733 O. S., Page 56
It is ordered that John Stoell and James Arnold be added to William Hagood's Gang --

7 March 1733 O. S., Page 57
Upon the Petition of Henry Rottenbury it is ordered that he be Exempted from Clearing the Highways --

4 April 1734 O. S., Page 61
Michael Wall is appointed Overseer of the high Way between Hicks's ford on Maherrin in the County Line and that all tyths that formerly belonged to it assist in Clearing and Keeping the Same --

2 May 1734 O. S., Page 65
Grand Jury Presentments
...also against William Kymball Overseer of the Road from the flatt Rock of the Reedy Creek to Christiana ffort for not Keeping the Road in Repair according to Law ...

6 June 1734 O. S., Page 66
ffrancis Wray is appointed Overseer of a Road from the old trading path to the Road by Benjaming Kymball's and that all the Male Labouring Tyths from John Thomsons up to the fort assist in Clearing the Same --

6 June 1734 O. S., Page 66
Daniel Hicks is appointed Surveyor of a Road from Roger Smith's fford up to Chamberlains Road and that all the Tyths from Arthur Harris up to Col°. Allen's Quarter are Ordered to assist in Clearing the Same --

7 November 1734 O. S., Page 71
Upon the petition of Roger Tillman it is ordered that the Surveyor of the Road to the bridge near the Lower cut banks assisted by his Gang Make a Cosway to the S^d. Bridge.

7 November 1734 O. S., Page 72
William Hogan is appointed Overseer of a Road from his ford over the North fork of Roanoake to [missing] ford on Maherrin and that all the Male Labouring Tythes above [missing] Creek Except John Williams assist in Clearing the Same --

7 November 1734 O. S., Page 72
Richard Ledbetter is appointed Overseer of a bridle Way from Quarrel Swap at Henry Ledbetters old path to the old Westward ford on Maherrin River, & from thence the Straitest way into Tatum's Road and that all the Male Labouring Tyths between the great Creek & Matt Edwards he being included William Kymball Thomas Bailes Richard Bryan & John Bartholomew assist in Clearing the Same --

5 December 1734 O. S., Page 73
Lawrence House is appointed Overseer of the old Road from Allens Mill to the Maherrin Road and that Thomas Laurence, John Dunn, William Melton, Francis Renn, Robert Page, and his Tyths assist in Clearing the Same --

5 December 1734 O. S., Page 74
Samuel Harwell & Patrick Smith are appointed to Keep the Bridge clear from Loggs and that the due performance thereof Shall Exempt them from the Clearing of Roads --

6 December 1734 O. S., Page 76
County Levy
To Paul Sears for his proportionable part of the building a bridge at the upper cut banks to be paid out of the Money arising from the tobb.° due by Wolves heads   [blank in book]

6 February 1734 O. S., Page 82
James Mackdaniel is appointed Surveyor of the highway from Maherrin River near Mizes to the Main Road instead of William Maclin gent and that all the Male Labouring Tyths in his former order assist in Clearing the Same.

6 February 1734 O. S., Page 82
James Oliver is appointed Overseer of the Church Road from the great Creek and that all the tyths in James M^c.Daniel's order assist in Clearing the Same --

6 February 1734 O. S., Page 82
John Humphris is appointed Surveyor of the Highway from this Court House to Sturgeon Run and that all the Tyths within his old bounds (Except Harrison's quarter) assist in clearing the Same.

6 February 1734 O. S., Page 82
Matthew Creed is appointed Surveyor in Stead of Clement Read gent on the Road from Robert Humphris's to the Church and that the Same gang in Read's order assist him in Clearing the Same.

6 February 1734 O. S., Page 82
Nicholas Laniergent. is appointed to be overseer of a briddle way from his house to this Court House and tha Thomas Lloyd Robert Gee and James Gordle be Exempted two Days from Working on other Roads to Assist him in Clearing the Same --

6 February 1734 O. S., Page 82
Natt Edwards is Appointed Surveyor of the High Way from Richard Ledbetter's on Rattle Snake Swamp to the Western ford on Maherrin and over ye River the nearest and best Way into the Road that leads from the ffort over the lower Lower Cut banks of Nottoway and that all the Labouring Tyths above his House and below the fort on the South Side Maherrin assist in Clearin the Same leaving Henry Ledbetter to his Choice --

6 February 1734 O. S., Page 83
It is ordered that it be henceforth a Rule of this Court that there be no orders made Concerning Roads only in the Months of March and October --

3 April 1735 O. S., Page 85
Arthur Harris is Appointed Overseer of the Road instead of Daniel Hix and it is ordered that his Gang in the S^d Hix's Order Assist in Clearing the Same --

1 May 1735 O. S., Page 90
Grand Jury Presentments
… Patrick [missing] for not keeping the Road in Repare …

… Samuel Chamberlain for not keeping the Road in Repair from the Westward ford to the old Westward Path …

7 August 1735 O. S., Page 101
It is ordered that John Adcocke Assist Samuel Harwell to take care and keep the lower cutt-bank Bridge from being injur'd by Loggs which may be Lodg against the Same and if he perform his duty therein he is to be Exempted from Clearing the high Ways --

7 August 1735 O. S., Page 102
It is ordered that Charles Kimball be Overseer of the High Way in the Room of Hosea Tapley --

7 August 1735 O. S., Page 110
Byrd Lanier is Appointed Overseer of the Road from Nottoway Road to Shining Creek and that all the hands that use to Work upon the Said Road below Shining Creek Assist in Clearing the Same --

7 August 1735 O. S., Page 110
Daniel Nantz is appointed Overseer of the Roanoak Road from the Ridge out instead of Thomas Wilson --

7 August 1735 O. S., Page 111
Upon the petition of William Davis to turn a Road that was prejudicial to his Plantation on the South Side of Roanoak River it is ordered that he turn the Same to the best advantage --

7 August 1735 O. S., Page 111
It is ordered that William Blaikley's Tyths and Thomas Lanier be added to Clement Read's Order

2 October 1735 O. S., Page 111
Upon the Petition of Several of the Inhabitants of Brunswick County for the building of a bridge over Nottoway River at or Near the place Called Sweades the Court Considering on the Same Ordered that Henry Embry, John Wall, & John Duke gent or any two of them treat and Consult with the Justices of Surry Court at their next Court Concerning the Same --

2 October 1735 O. S., Page 111
Mason Bishop is appointed overseer of the Road leading from Humphris's Church Path to the great Creek near Mason Bishop's and that Henry Morris & his Tyths & James Parish & his Tyths Assist in Clearing the Same --

2 October 1735 O. S., Page 111
William Maclin gent. has leave to Clear a bridle way from his House into the Church Road and that he be Exempted two days from further Service --

2 October 1735 O. S., Page 111
Richard Huckabey is appointed Overseer of the Road from the old Brunswick line up to the Reedy Creek instead of Hosea Tapley

6 November 1735 O. S., Page 112
William Wynne gent. is appointed Overseer of a Road from Jones Ford over waqua into the Court House Road between Sturgeon Runn & Waqua and that Henry Simmons William Jones Henry Jones Hix Jones & Lewellin Jones & their Tyths Assist in Clearing the Same --

6 November 1735 O. S., Page 113
Grand Jury Presentments
Matthew Creed for not keeping the Road in Repair ...

6 November 1735 O. S., Page 113
Henry Morris is Appointed overseer of a Road from Chunketapusso to the Reedy Creek and that Col.[1] Harrison's Col.[1] Allen's and Robert Munford's Tyths Assist in Clearing the Same --

6 November 1735 O. S., Page 113
Joseph Colson is appointed Overseer of a Road from the Island ford to Butcher's Road and that Munfords Powels, and Walkers Tyths Assist in Clearing the Same --

4 December 1735 O. S., Page 114
Samuel Chamberlain is appointed Overseer of a Road from Chamberlains ford over Maherrin to the Governours Road and that the hands in his former Order Assist in Clearing the Same --

5 December 1735 O. S., Page 115
A Petition of Several of the Inhabitants of Brunswick County for the building of a bridge over Nottoway River at or near the place Called Sweades was brought into Court and the Same being Read together with the Severall Subscriptions the Court ordered that Henry Embry, John Wall & John Duke gent or any two of them Should treat with the justices of Surry County Court Concerning the building of the Same --

5 February 1735 O. S., Page 119
Upon the Petition of Robert Hicks leave is granted him to keep a ferry over Maherrin River at the place Called Hiks's Ford and it is ordered that the following rates be allowed Viz^t for Every Hogshead Tobacco & Cart one Shilling & three pence, for a Man & Horse four pence and for a Man only four pence --

6 February 1735 O. S., Page 120
John Douglass is appointed Overseer of a Road from Chamberlains Ford over Maherrin to the Governours Road and that all the hands in Chamberlains former order assist in Clearing the Same --

6 February 1735 O. S., Page 121
John Day is Appointed Overseer of the Road instead of James Oliver --

6 February 1735 O. S., Page 122
On the presentment of the Grand Jury against Matthew Creed for not keeping the Road in repair the Said Matthew thereupon Making it appear to the Contrary it is ordered that the Same be dismist --

4 March 1735 O. S., Page 124
Abraham Browne is appointed Overseer of the Road that leads from the Court House to the Reedy Creeke Instead of John Rose --

4 March 1735 O. S., Page 124
William Stroud is appointed Overseer of the Road from Miles's Creek to John Butcher's and that all the Male Tyths between Allens Creek and Butchers Creek on both Sides Roanoak River Assist in Clearing the Same --

4 March 1735 O. S., Page 124
George Hicks is ordered and Appointed an Overseer of the Road Instead of Henry Wych --

4 March 1735 O. S., Page 124
Henry Embry John Wall and John Duke gent. or any two of them are Appointed to treat with the Justices of the Court of Surry County Concerning the building of a bridge over Nottoway River at the place Called Sweads ford --

4 March 1735 O. S., Page 124
John Douglass is Appointed Overseer of a Road from Doctor Irby's to the old Westward Path instead of Samuel Chamberlain --

7 October 1736 O. S., Page 137
Henry Embry, John Wall, & Batt Peterson or any one of them are appointed & desired to treat with the Court of Isle of Wight County Concerning the Building of a Bridge over Maherrin River at or near Benjamin Chapman Donaldson's --

7 October 1736 O. S., Page 138
James Matthews Humphris is appointed Overseer of the Road instead of Rober Humphris --

7 October 1736 O. S., Page 138
Richard Burch gent. is appointed Overseer of the Nottoway to Sturgeon Runn Instead of John Wall --

7 October 1736 O. S., Page 138
Cornelius Cargill is appointed Overseer of the Road from Roanoake River Near Hogans to the Long Branch without Buckshorn Instead of William Hogan and that all the persons within the Said bounds Assist in Clearing the Same --

7 October 1736 O. S., Page 138
Samuel Holmes is Appointed Overseer of the Road from Maherrin River near Walters's to the Long Branch without Buckhorn and that all the persons within the Said bounds Assist in Clearing the Same --

7 October 1736 O. S., Page 138
It is ordered that Joseph Colson Clear the Road to the Wolf Pit at Coleman's Path and that Patrick Damm Clear from thence to Maherrin --

7 October 1736 O. S., Page 138
John Jackson is appointed Overseer instead of John Douglass from the Reedy Creeke to Maherrin and Graves Eaves and William Eaves and David Bails be added to the former Order --

7 October 1736 O. S., Page 138
Henry Embry, John Wall & John Duke or any one of them is appointed to treat with the Court of Surry about the building of Bridge over Nottoway River at or near the place Called Sweads --

7 October 1736 O. S., Page 138
Drury Stith gent appointed Overseer of a Road from his Mill into the Court Road and that Thomas Couch Senr. Thomas Couch ju^r. and William Couch Assist in Clearing the Same --

4 November 1736 O. S., Page 141
William Moseley is appointed Overseer of the High Way that leads from the County line near the lizard Creek down to the Road on Rattle Snake and that John Moseley Thomas Lych, John Hulin Richard Smith, and William Rough and they Tyths assist in Clearing the Same --

2 December 1736 O. S., Page 143
William Roark is appointed Surveyor of the High Way from M^r. Walls Road about half a Mile from the River to the Beaver pond Creek and that George Brewer Senr Howell Brewer, William Brewer, William Wise, Senr. William Wise ju^r Thomas Powell, Thomas Powell ju^r, Douglass Powell, William Powell, John Powell, John Rook, Joseph Heathcock, John Brewer, John Jeffers, Ninian Mitchell, Lanier Brewer, Charles Brady, John Wise, James Turner, John Cooke & Nathaniel Carter assis in Clearing the Same --

3 February 1736 O. S., Page 147
Nathaniel Edwards is Appointed Surveyor of the Road from Smith's Ford to the Church Road instead of Arthur Harris and that the tyths belonging to Coll Allen and M^r. Benjamin Harrison be added to the former Gang --

3 February 1736 O. S., Page 149
Robert Sanford is appointed Surveyor of a Road from flatt Rock Creek by Mason Bishops into M^r. Burch's Road and that all the Tyths belonging to John Edloe Henry Edloe Edward Broadnax & William Kelley assist in Clearing the Same --

7 April 1737 O. S., Page 153
Samuell Crawley is appointed Overseer of the Road from Burch's Road that Leads towards Flatt Rock Instead of Clement Read --

2 June 1737 O. S., Page 155
On the motion of Nicholas Lanier gent who represented to the Court that the lower Cutt bank Bridge Stood in great need of repair it is thereupon ordered that he be Appointed to agree with the Workman and Employ them in repairing the Same --

2 June 1737 O. S., Page 155
Francis Wray is appointed overseer of the Road from the North Ford one the North Side of Maherrin to Rattle Snake instead of Nathaniel Edwards --

3 June 1737 O. S., Page 159
John Wall gent came into Court and made the following Reports of his proceedings on the order of this Court, who appointed him to treat with the Justices of Surry Court and the Justices of Isle of Wight Court to build bridges over Nottoway River and Maherrin River according to the Severall Orders Viz^t.

In obedience to an Order of Brunswick County Court dated the Seventh day of October anno Dom MDCCXXXVI,

I have treated with the Court of Isle of Wight County about the building a Bridge over Maherrin River at Benjamin Chapman Donaldson's and that Court agreeing that a Bridge Should be Built there according to the Tenor of that Order I did together With the gentlemen Appointed by that Court agree with Thomas Parsons to build a Bridge at the place afsd for fifty Six pounds Curr^t. Money be Keeping the Same in repair Seven Years and in Case the Bridge Should at anytime in the Said Space be rendred impassable the Said Parsons is to Keep a ferry at the Said place free for the Transportations of all persons 'till the Same Shall be again repaired, the Money for building the Said Bridge to be paid to the S^d: Parsons in June MDCCXXXVII

J Wall

In obedience to an Order of Brunswick County Court Dated the Seventh day of October Anno Dom. MDCCXXXVI.

I have treated with the Court of Surry County about building a Bride over Nottoway River at Sweeds and that Court agreeing that a Bridge Should be built there according to the Tenor of that order I did together with the gentlemen appointed by that Court Agree with William Rose to Build a Bridge at the place afs^d for fifty five pounds Curr^t. Money he keeping the Same in Repair Seven Years the Money for building the Said Bridge being to be paid to the Said Rose in June MDCCXXXVIII.

J Wall

3 November 1737 O.S., Page 172
Upon the Petition of John Chapman and Setting forth in the Same the Conveniency and Necessitty of a bridge over the three Creeks at the most Convenient place near Coll^l. Allen's Mill it is thereupon ordered that John Wall, John Duke and Batt Peterson Employ workmen to Build the Same --

3 November 1737 O.S., Page 173
James Coleman is appointed Overseer in lieu of Patrick Dorum --

3 November 1737 O.S., Page 173
Upon the Petition of George Hix and Setting forth in the Same that he being overseer of the Road from Meherrin River to the Otter dams in Which Road the Bridge over the three Creeks being Rotten and the Company under him being unable to rebuild it the Court thereupon ordered that John Wall, John Duke & Batte Peterson Employ Workman to build a bridge over the Same --

3 November 1737 O.S., Page 173
Robert Humphris is Appointed Overseer of the Road from William Hogan's to the Ford over Stanton River near Munford's Plantation into Cargill's Road and that all the Male Tyths above Peter Mitchel assist in Clearing the Same --

3 November 1737 O. S., Page 174
James Matthews is appointed Surveyor of a Road from Wild Catt into Burch's Road and its ordered that James Matthews ju^r, Isaac Matthews, John Matthews, Charles Matthews, Richard Swanson, Edward Swanson, John Hilerease, William Reynolds, William Dishmall, John Jackson, William Reaves, Samuel Crawley, William Fletcher, Richard Smith, Griffin Humphris, John Browne, Capt Richard Jones Tyths, Richard Parr, and their Tyths Assist in Clearing the Same --

4 November 1737 O. S., Page 175
It is ordered that James Mackdaniels Gang Byrd Thomas Lanier's Gang and Robert Sanford's Gang meet William Maclin gent. when thereunto required in order to build bridges over the great Creek and Shining Creek --

4 November 1737 O. S., Page 175
John Hagood is appointed overseer of the High Way in Steed of William Hagood --

4 November 1737 O. S., Page 175
Michael Wall, Charles Stewart, Lawrence Hows & George Hix are appointed to lay of a Road from the old three Creek bridge on Hix's Road to Sweeds Bridge and that George Hix's gang & Lawrence Hows's Gangs Assist in Clearing the Same and that Coll^l. Harrison's Tyths of Sweeds be added to Rows's Gang --

2 December 1737 O. S., Page 183
County Levy
To Tobb^o Levied for Defraying the Charges of Building of three Bridges one over Maherrin, one over Nottoway and one over the three Creeks ... 4,000

2 February 1737 O. S., Page 184
Benjamin Chapman Donaldson is appointed Surveyor of the High Way down to the Bridge instead of James Halsy --

2 March 1737 O.S., Page 186
James Riggby is appointed Overseer of the Road instead of Matthew Creed who came into Court and Relinquished his authority thereto --

2 March 1737 O. S., Page 187
William Gower is appointed Overseer of that part of the Road that Richard Huckabey was appointed Overseer of who came into Court and relinquished his authority thereto --

6 April 1738 O. S., Page 190
John Wall & Batt Peterson gent are appointed and desired to view & Receive the bridge that John Maclin (who was imploy'd to build the Same over the three Creeks) has lately performed --

3 August 1738 O. S., Page 202
William Gunn is appointed Overseer of the Road instead of John Humphris --

7 September 1738 O. S., Page 204
Ordered that George Dearden be appointed Surveyor of the King's High Way from Nottoway River to Sturgeon Run in the lieu of Richard Burch Gent --

7 September 1738 O. S., Page 204
Ordered that Richard Ledbetter, James Uupchurch, Richard Smith & William Uupchurch be taken from ffrancis Wrays Gang and that they be added to William Moseleys Gang --

7 September 1738 O. S., Page 204
Ordered that John Wray be Overseer of ye Highway instead of Francis Wray --

7 September 1738 O. S., Page 210
Ordered that John Wall, John Duke, Batt Peterson or any of them agree with Workman to build a bridge over the three Creeks at the old Road

2 November 1738 O. S., Page 215
John Cole is appointed of the Roanoake Road from the Ridge out instead of Thomas Willson --

2 November 1738 O. S., Page 215
Nicholas Brewer is appointed Overseer of the Road instead of William Acock

2 November 1738 O. S., Page 215
Robert Coock is appointed Overseer of a Road from the bridge at Cooks Creek to Butchers Road and that Thomas Stephens John Hewin Joseph Hart John Cole John Nipper Ju{r} Thomas Crawford David Allen John Roberts And Alexander Hayes Assis in Clearing the Same --

2 November 1738 O. S., Page 215
Nicholas Lanier Gent is appointed Overseer of the Road from the Ready Creek to the Lower Cut banks instead of Charles King --

2 November 1738 O. S., Page 215
William Ghent is Appointed Overseer of the Road instead of Cornelius Cargill

3 November 1738 O. S., Page 216
It is ordered that Lewis Parham William Acock & Michael Wall or Either two of them Shall lay out a Road from Sweeds Bridge to the Otterdam Bridge the mos Convenient in their Judgments, And it is also Ordered that George Hicks's Gang and Lawrence Hows's Gang Clear the Same --

3 November 1738 O. S., Page 216
Grand Jury Presentments
...the Overseer of the Road from Col{l}. Byrd's quarter at Maherrin to Roanoake Chappel for not keeping the Road in Repair ...

...the overseer of the upper part of the Road from James Mize's to the fork of Roanoak ...

...the Overseer of the Road on the North Side of Maherrin from Capt. Hicks's Ford to Charles Stewart's Shop --

1 February 1738 O. S., Page 218
John Boucher is appointed Overseer of the Road instead of Willaim Stroud --

1 February 1738 O. S., Page 218
Josias Randle is appointed Overseer in lieu of Samuel Crawley --

1 February 1738 O. S., Page 218
Moses Dunkley is appointed Overseer of the Road in the Room of William Gunn --

1 February 1738 O. S., Page 220
John Wall gent. is appointed Overseer of a Road from Sweeds Bridge the most Convenient Way into the old Maherrin Road and that Charles Stewart, John Cate Charles Dinkins, James Dinkins, Thomas Sandford, John Gardiner and the Tyths under him assist in Clearing the Same --

1 February 1738 O. S.. Page 220
Henry Embry John Wall & Drury Stith Gent. or Either of them is appointed to Solicit the Court of Prince George to Assist in building the Bridge at the Lower cut banks and to agree with workmen accordingly --

2 February 1738 O. S., Page 222
John Evans is appointed Overseer of the Road from Chunketapusso to the Reedy Creek instead of Henry Morris --

2 February 1738 O. S., Page 227
On the presentment of the Grand Jury against George Hix for not keeping the Road in Repair the Said Hix came into Court and gave reasons why the clearing of the Road was omitted the Court Considering of the Same ordered that the Suit be dismist

2 February 1738 O. S., Page 227
Our Sovereign Lord the King against James Coleman Overseer of the Highway for not keeping the Same in Repair the Said Coleman came into Court and gave reasons why the Same was omitted, the Court Considering of the Same ordered that the Suit be dismist --

2 February 1738 O. S., Page 227
Cornelius Cargill was presented by the grand jury for not keeping the High way in repair (he being overseer of the Same) a Subpena was thereupon Issued for the Said Cargill to appear befor the Court and Shew Cause why the Same was Neglected and thereupon the Said Cargill appearing at the Barr gave Such Reasons as was thought by the Court Sufficient to Exclude him from fine or penalty therefore the Court ordered that the Suit be dismist --

1 March 1738 O. S., Page 231
Benjamin Harrison is appointed Overseer of the Road from the great Creek to the Church instead of John Day --

1 March 1738 O .S., Page 231
Lazarus Williams is appointed Overseer of a Road from a Blaz'd White Oake on the Ridge between Nottoway & Maherrin Rivers between Thomas Jones & Toby's to Cook's House on Hounds Creek and that Richard Williams Stephen Dampier, Godfrey Brown, Warwick, Toby, Edward Calwell William Hawkins John Blackstone Lazarus Williams & Thomas Jones assist in Clearing the Same together with their Tyths

1 March 1738 O .S., Page 231
Robert Henry Dyer is appointed overseer of a Road from Cook's House on Hounds Creek to Nottoway River Below the fork and that Charles Parrish William Rivers Thomas Jones and Jonathan Moate with their Tyths assist in Clearing the Same --

1 March 1738 O. S., Page 232
John Fennel is appointed Overseer of the Road instead of Benjamin Chapman Donaldson

3 May 1739 O. S., Page 240
Ordered that the Respective Surveyors of the high Ways where two or more Cross Roads meet, forthwith do Erect or Cause to be Erected in the most Convenient Place, where Such Ways Joyn. a Stone or Post with Inscriptions thereon, in large Letters, directing to the most noted Place, to which Each of the Said joining Roads Leads: according to the late Act of Assembly --

3 May 1739 O. S., Page 240
On the motion of Cornelius Keith Leave is granted him to keep a Ferry over Roanoak River from his own Landing below the Horse ford to Alexander's Landing and that he keep for that purpose a good and Sufficient Strong flatt flatt fourteen foot and a half in her bottom and Six foot upon her beam and that he Receive for his ferriage Six pence for Man and Six pence for a Horse and as the Law directs for Wheel Carriages, two pence for Every Hogg and four pence for Each of the Cattle Kind, also ordered that he give bond and Security for the Same --

3 May 1739 O. S., Page 242
Grand Jury Presentments

. . . the Overseer of the lower part of the Road that leads from Henry Cooks Road to the Bridge that leads over Maherrin River and M^r. Donaldson's --

. . . William Gent for not keeping his Road Clear'd as the Law Directs.

3 August 1739 O. S., Page 261
William Gent was presented by the Grand jury for not keeping the Road in repair therefore a Subpena Was Issued to Cause the Said Gent to appear before the Justices of our Said Court which was accordingly done and returned Executed by the Sher and the Said Gent appearing at the barr and there Setting forth that he was not in a Capacity to Cause the Same to be Cleared as being at that time in the Custody of the Sheriff that Court upon Herein of his Alegation ordered that the Suit be dismist --

6 December 1739 O. S., Page 269
Joseph Dunman is appointed Overseer of the Road instead of Henry Bedingfield

6 December 1739 O. S., Page 269
Richard Ledbetter Ju^r is appointed Overseer instead of William Mobley

6 December 1739 O. S., Page 270
Henry Embry & John Wall gent or Either of them is appointed to treat with the Justices of Prince George County of and Concerning the building of a Bridge over Nottoway River at the Lower Cut Banks, and also to agree with Workmen to build the Same --

6 December 1739 O. S., Page 270
Samuel Manning is appointed Overseer of the Road in lieu of James Coleman Who relinquished the Same --

6 December 1739 O. S., Page 270
Ordered that a Road be Cleared from Waqua to Nottoway River to meet the Road from Amelia Court House as the Path now goes by Thomas Jones's Mill and that the Persons Convenient Assist in Clearing the Same and also that Charles Matthews is appointed Overseer thereof --

6 December 1739 O. S., Page 270
Hinckey Mabry, John Pettway Samuel Russell, William Smith, John Brooks, Merridiths Tyths, John Goodwynn, George Mabry, William King the Colledge Tyths and Robert Reynard and their Tyths Assist Hinckey Mabrey in Clearing a Road from Nottoway River where Thomas Jones had a fish Dam to the old Road Near Duke's Race Paths --

6 December 1739 O. S., Page 273
John Wray is appointed Overseer of the Road the Most Convenient Way from the old fort Road into the Westward Road and that his old Gang is ordered to Clear the Same --

7 February 1739 O. S., Page 286
John Twitty is appointed Surveyor of a Road from Talbotts Plantation on little Roanoak to the Road between Embry's & Thomas Jones's Plantations on the Nap of Reads Creek and that Matthew Talbott, John Jinkins William Baughstick, William Lax, William Williamson, Evan Rease, John Bently Richard Jones, Thomas Winford, John Hurt & Hugh Boston assist in Clearing the Same. --

6 March 1739 O. S., Page 298
Henry Jones is appointed Overseer of the Road instead of William Wynce Gent --

6 March 1739 O. S., Page 298
Ordered that Edward Green be Surveyor of a Road from Peterson's Ford on ffountains Creek the most Convenient Way to Donaldson's Bridge and that Peter Wych, John Tuke, Henry Ivey, Joseph Parks, Edward Meachams William Ezel, William Southerland, John Batts, Robert Southerland James Adkins, William Barter, James Jordan, William Jordan, Alex^r. Southerland, Mary Jordan, Belian Possey Assist With their Tyths in Clearing the Same --

6 March 1739 O. S., Page 298
William Collier is appointed Overseer of the Road from Benjamin Harrison's Mill the Most Convenient Way to the Court House Road the Nearest Way towards the Cut Bank Bridge And that Ambrose Jackson, Thomas Jackson, Edward Goodrich, Thomas Denton, Edward Denton, Stephen Sissons William Sissons, Joseputh Shearing, John Shearing, John Peoples, Peter Simmons, William Gower, George Harper and their Tyths Assist in Clearing the Same -- & Thomas [illegible]ssum & his Tyths

6 March 1739 O. S., Page 299
John Duke gent is appointed Overseer of a Road from his Race Paths the most Convenient Way to the lower Cut bank Bridge and that John Cooke William Moore, John Harwell, Francis Lett, George Tillman, Roger Tillman, James Wortham and their Tyths Assist in Clearing the Same --

6 March 1739 O. S., Page 299
George Hix is appointed Overseer of a Road from Maj^r Benjamin Harrison's Mill over Reaves's Swamp to meet the Isle of Wight Road from Coals's old Feild and that Hubbert Farrill William Lucas and Maj^r Ben^J Harrison's Tyths Assist in Clearing the Same --

3 April 1740 O. S., Page 302
Edward Swanson is appointed Overseer of the Road instead of James Matthews who Relinquished the Same --

3 April 1740 O. S., Page 302
Ordered that Francis Elledge be added to Richard Ledbetter's Gang --

5 June 1740 O. S., Page 304
On the Petition of William Jenkins setting forth "That the Petitioner lived on the South Side of Roanoke River opposite to the Ferry lately put up at the Horse Foard and had a convenient Boat to transport Men and Horses over the said River" And therefore praying "That the Court would permit him to keep a Ferry he being ready to give Bond & C" It is Order'd That the same be Rejected --

3 July 1740 O. S., Page 327
Order'd; That a Road be clear'd beginning near the mouth of Turnip Creek and to run as far as the Ridge between Appomattox and Roanoak Rivers and that all the Titheable Persons in this County above the mouth of Cub Creek and on both sides the said Rivers being convenient assist in clearing the same And that William Fuqua be appointed Overseer thereof.

4 September 1740 O. S., Page 345
John Chapman Gent is appointed and desired to acquaint the Court of Isle of Wight County that Thomas Parsons refuses to keep the bridge called Donaldson's in repair which is in immediate want thereof and to desire that Court to join with this in treating with Workmen to perform the same.

2 October 1740 O. S., Page 374
John Chapman Gentleman reported That "in Obedience to an Order of this Court he had acquainted the Isle of Wight Court in a proper manner of that Order Which Court had deputed John Parsons Joseph Gray Howel Edmunds and John Dunkley Gentlemen to treat with gentlemen to be deputed by this Court to agree with undertakers for the Repairing and keeping in repair the Bridge over Maherrin River commonly known by the Name of Donaldson's Bridge" Whereupon this Court doth appoint John Wall Michael Wall and John Peterson Gent or either of them to agree in conjunction with the Gentlemen nominated by the Court of Isle of Wight with undertakers accordingly --

2 October 1740 O. S., Page 384
Order'd That Edward Pennington be appointed Surveyor of the Road in the room of Joseph Dunman deced --

6 November 1740 O. S., Page 398
Order'd That the first Tithable Persons who were appointed to Clear the Road from Sneed's towards the Courthouse attend William Gower the present Surveyor of the s^d. Road at such times as he shall judge necessary for keeping the same in Repair according to Law --

5 March 1740 O. S., Page 405
John Duke Gentleman is appointed Surveyor of the Roads in the room of William Gower and Hinchey Mabry

5 March 1740 O. S., Page 405
Seth Petty Poole is appointed Overseer of the Road in the room of George Dearden

5 March 1740 O. S., Page 405
On the Petition of several of the Inhabitants of this County leave is granted them to clear a bridle way from Tabbs Quarter on Waqua the most convenient way to the Church and Thomas Lenoir is appointed Overseer thereof --

5 March 1740 O. S., Page 406
Upon the Petition of Martha Alexander Setting forth "That having Land on the South Side of Roanok River opposite to Cornelius Keith's Land she humbly desires an Order of this Court Licensing her to keep a Ferry from her Land over the River to Cornelius Keith's Landing she being ready to

give Security as the Law directs" It is Order'd That the Clerk prepare a Licence for her accordingly upon her giving such Security --

5 March 1740 O. S., Page 406
Upon the Petition of Christopher DeGraffenreidt leave is granted him to clear a Road from his Quarter to great Nottoway River in this County the most convenient way a little above Fisher's Quarter --

5 March 1740 O. S., Page 406
Upon the Petition of Thomas Winford John Austin Richard Austin and Thomas Connoway Order'd That they assist in clearing and keeping the Road in repair whereof William Fuqua is appointed Surveyor --

2 April 1741 O. S., Page 407
Order'd That William Hampton Robert Briggs Mr Smith Thomas Lenoir Thomas Nunn William Edwards Philemon Bowers James Love Charles Valentine with their Male labouring Tithables and the Male labouring Tithables of Catherine Blaikley Widow assist Josias Randle Surveyor of the Road from Burch's Road to Briggs's Road in clearing and keeping the said Road according to Law --

2 April 1741 O. S., Page 407
Order'd That Robert Dyer Charles Parrish Thomas Jones [illegible] Matthews Matthew Matthews William Rivers and John Drue with their Male labouring Tithables assist Charles Matthews Surveyor of the Road order'd to be cleared from Waqua at Briggs's to the Amelia Road at Nottoway River in clearing and keeping the same according to Law --

2 April 1741 O. S., Page 408
Order'd That Thomas Person be appointed Surveyor of the Road from Taylor's Landing to the Road whereof John Fennel is Surveyor and that his Male labouring Tithables with the Male labouring Tithables of Henry Taylor and Charles Campbell assist in clearing and keeping the same according to Law --

2 April 1741 O. S., Page 408
Order'd that a new bridge be built over Maherrin River at Donaldson's and that John Wall Batt Peterson and Michael Wall Gent or anyone of them treat with the Court of Isle of Wight County concerning the same --

2 April 1741 O. S., Page 408
Order'd That Henry Morris be appointed Surveyor of the Highway instead of Abraham Brown --

3 April 1741 O. S., Page 423
John Chapman Gent is appointed and desired to acquaint the County Court of Surry that the bridge over Nottoway River at Sweeds has been carried away by a late fresh and that this Court expects they will join with them in taking proper measures to have the same rebuilt --

7 May 1741 O. S., Page 429
Order'd That Thomas Lenoir Overseer of the Road from the Waqua to the Courthouse be discharged from working on the Road whereof Josias Randle is Overseer --

7 May 1741 O. S., Page 429
Order'd That a new Road be cleared from the main Road near Robinson's on Maherrin and thence on the Ridge as Young's goes to the Country line And that Francis Ellidge Jeremy Ellidge George Robinson John McAvail Daniel Carrel Hugh Daniel Richard Hawkins and Humphry Hughy with their Male labouring Tithables assist John Steed who is hereby appointed Surveyor of the Said road in clearing the same --

7 May 1741 O. S., Page 446

Upon the Presentment of the Grand Jury against William Gent Surveyor of the Road from Allen's Creek to the Fork of Roanoak for not keeping the said Road in Repair This day came the Attorney of our Lord the King and Saith That for reasons appearing to him he will not further Prosecute against the said William upon the Presentment aforesaid Therefore It is Consider'd that the said William go thereof without Day --

Brunswick County Order Book 2

2 July 1741 O. S., Page 6
For Reasons appearing to this Court Order'd that the Petition of several of the Inhabitants of this County for a Bridge over Allens Creek where the Road called Butchers Road crossed the said Creek be Rejected --

6 August 1741 O. S., Page 10
Order'd that the Surveyor of the Road called the Roan oak Road turn the s^d Road So as to Cross Maherrin River at the Ford where its common to ride over --

6 August 1741 O. S.. Page 24
Order'd that Thomas Sadler be appointed Surveyor of the Road in the room of Moses Dunkley

6 August 1741 O. S., Page 24
Orderd that Amos Timms be appointed Surveyor of the Road in commonly called the Lower Cut Bank Road in the room of Henry Morris --

3 September 1741 O. S., Page 28
Order'd that John Cargill be appointed Surveyor of the Road in the room of William Gent

3 September 1741 O. S.. Page 28
Order'd that John Mitchell be appointed Surveyor of the Road in the room of John Boucher

3 September 1741 O. S., Page 28
Upon the Petition of several of the Inhabitants of this County Order'd that a Road be clear'd from Twitty's Road a little below the mouth of Ledbetters Creek the most convenient way to Nottoway River and that John Winningham be appointed Surveyor thereof --

3 September 1741 O. S., Page 29
Upon the Petition of Robert Southerland and others Order'd that a Road be cleared from Jack Swamp the most convenient way to the bridge that is building below the mouth of Fountains Creek and that all the male labouring Tithables on the South side of the said Creek and below the mouth of the said Swamp assist William Jordan (who is hereby appointed Surveyor of the said Road) in clearing and keeping the same according to Law --

3 September 1741 O. S., Page 29
For Reasons appearing to this Court Order'd That a Road be Clear'd from Col^o. Richard Randolphs Quarter at the mouth of Little Roan oak til it meets the Road Order'd to be clear'd by Amelia County Court to the Ridge that divides this County from that and that Charle Jenkens and his son

John Twitty Thomas Jones Jonathan Horsford John Calwell Evan Rees John Maddin Mathew Talbot Samuel Horsford with their Male labouring Tithables and the Male labouring Tithables of the said Randolp Josep Moreton and John Coles assist Andrew Moreman (who is hereby appointed surveyor of the said Road in clearing and keeping the same according to Law.

3 September 1741 O. S., Page 29
Order'd that John Ezwell Ezekiel Matthews Edward Henlin Anthony Tann James Hicks Joseph Hicks Pilip Roberts William Goss Daniel Murfey Josia Floyd William Middleton and David Nantz with their Male labouring Tithables keep the Road from Flatt Creek to Maherrin River in repair according to Law and that the said Daniel Nantz be appointed Surveyor thereof --

1 October 1741 O. S., Page 35
Order'd that Ralph Jackson be appointed Surveyor of the Highway from the Reedy Creek to Edwards's Path and that Thomas Jackson Peter Tatum Joseph Tatum Thomas Bull Edward Robinson William Kimball John Moore David Sinclair Henry Jackson John Hix and China Tatum with their Male labouring Tithables assist the said Ralph in keeping the same according to Law

1 October 1741 O. S., Page 35
On the Motion of John Hall Gent leave is granted him to turn the Road called the Trading Path that runs by his Plantation

1 October 1741 O. S., Page 35
Order'd that Henry Rottenbury Francis Troublefeild John Nipper James Nipper John Platt William Goss Robert BrooksRobert Allen Thomas Calford Humphry Hewey Philip Roberts John Chavas Richard Rottenbury clear the Road from Cockes Creek to Butchers Road whereof Robert Cooke is appointed Overseer

1 October 1741 O. S., Page 35
Upon the Petition of Several of the Inhabitants of this County leave is granted them to clear a bridle Path from Richard Woods Plantation the most convenient way into the Road by Mason Bishops and It is Order'd that the Male labouring Tithables belonging to Jases Parrish Henry Morris Thomas Spell Edward Cordle and John Dren clear the same and that the said Mason be appointed Surveyor thereof

1 October 1741 O. S., Page 35
Henry Embry and Richard Burch Gent are appointed to treat in conjunction with Such Gentleman as shall be Nominated by the Court of Princes George County with workman to repair the bridge over Nottoway River called the Upper Cut Bank Bridge

5 November 1741 O. S., Page 51
Memorandum that the Court is Satisfied with agreement made by the Gentleman nominated by this Court and the Court of Prince George County with W[m]. Bressie concerning the Rebuilding the Bridge over Nottoway River commonly called the Lower Cut bank Bridge

5 March 1741 O. S., Page 105
Ordered That a Road be cleared from Cargills Foard upon Staunton River to the convenientest Foard upon Bannister river & that Robert Humphries be appointed Overseer thereof

5 March 1741 O. S., Page 105
Ordered that John Cargill clear the Road whereof he is appointed Overseer so as meet the Road to be cleared from Cargill Ford on Staunton River to the convenientest Ford on Bannister River

1 April 1742 O. S., Page 106
Ordered that James Rigsby be appointed Surveior of the Road in the room of Josias Randle

1 April 1742 O. S., Page 107
Ordered that two bridges be Built over Maherrin River in this County the one at or near Hixs Ford & the other at or near the Ford at Byrds Quarter and that the Sherif give public notice that the said Bridge is to be let here the next Court and that George Wallton Nicholas Lanier and Michael Wall Gent or any two of them agree with workmen to build the said Bridges & that they be built Sixteen feet wide

1 April 1742 O. S., Page 107
It being represented to this Court that the persons who undertook to build the Bridges over Nottoway and Maherin Rivers at Sweeds and Donaldsons have failed in their Agreements Ordered that John Wall Gent be appointed & desir[d]. to put the said undertakers Bond in execution

1 April 1742 O. S., Page 107
Ordered that Michael Wall Gent have liberty to turn the Road whereof he is Surveior over any part of Fountains Creek he thinks convenient

1 April 1742 O. S., Page 107
Upon the Petition of Several of the Inhabitants of this County praying that a bridge may be built over Waqua Creek at the charge of the County It appearing that there is no occasion to burthen the County with the said Charge Ordered that the said Petition be rejected

Note: The remainder of the orders for 1742, as well as those for 1743, 1744 and January 1745 do not appear, although the order books are continuously numbered.

Brunswick County Order Book 3

6 February 1745 O. S., Page 10
On the Motion of Michael Wall Gent leave is granted him to alter that part of the Road called Cooke's Road which runs round his Cornfield so that the same be made convenient & Passable.

6 March 1745 O. S., Page 18
Order'd that Benjamin Harrison be appointed Surveyor of the High Ways from the Horse Ford Ferry to Cock's Creek and John Nipper from the S^d. Creek to Jeneto.

6 March 1745 O. S., Page 18
On the Motion of Richard Taliaferro Gent leave is granted him to turn the Road that runs thro' his Plantation in this County round the same so that such alteration be made convenient and Passable.

6 March 1745 O. S., Page 18
Order'd that Redman Fallon be appointed Surveyor of the High Ways from Fall Creek to the Country Line.

6 March 1745 O. S., Page 18
Order'd that William Johnson be appointed Surveyor of the High Ways in the room of William Huff and the said Huff in the room of John Steed.

6 March 1745 O. S., Page 19
Order'd That Seth Petty Poole, Robert Gee, James Gee Thomas Macclehaney Benjamin Winsley, Edward Giveins, Michael Mackey Willm. Macadow, William White and John Forest with their Male labouring Tithables clear the Road from the North Fork of Maherrin River into Cocke's Road whereof Saml: Willson is Surveior and keep the same in repair according to Law

6 March 1745 O. S., Page 19
Order'd That James Cunningham Robert Breakenridge Adam Breakenridge and Julius Nicholous with their Male labouring Tithables and the Male labouring Tithables in this County belonging to Lewis Burwell Gent clear the Road from the North Fork of Maherrin River to the Head of Butcher's Creek whereof John Twitty is Surveior and keep the same in repair according to Law.

6 March 1745 O. S., Page 19
On the Petition of James Gee and others for a Road from the most convenient Place on the branches of Reedy Creek to the Road that is cleared to Flatt Rock Order'd that the said Petition be referr'd to the Consideration of the next Court.

6 March 1745 O. S., Page 19
On the Petition of Mattox Mayes and others Order'd that leave be granted the pet^rs. to clear a Road from Joseph Mayes's New Ford on Stanton River the most convenient way to Turnip Creek below W^m. Cunningham's thence crossing the said Creek to Cubb Creek at Thos: Vernon's and thence crossing Cubb Creek as the old Road runs into Major Cole's Road and that the said Mattox be appointed Surveior thereof And it is a direction to other Surveiors that the clearing the S^d. Road is not to exempt the Pet^rs. or their Tithables from working on such other Roads as they respectively do at present

6 March 1745 O. S., Page 20
On the Petition of Richard Griffin and others Ordered that leave be granted the pet^rs. to clear a Road from Aaron's Creek to Robert Mitchell's Ford in this County and that the said Richard be appointed Surveior thereof.

6 March 1745 O. S., Page 20
Upon the Petition of John Mead and others praying an Order of this Court to oblige the Inhabitants on the head of Falling River from the Fork upwards to repair the Road from the head of Appomattox to Poplar Spring

against the North end the Long Mountain Order'd that the said Petition be Rejected.

6 March 1745 O. S., Page 20
Upon the Petition of Sundry the Inhabitants of this County & for reasons appearing to this Court Order'd that a Bridge be built over Maherrin River at or near Mize's Ford in this County And It is referr'd to William Madin and James Parrish Gent to employ Workmen to build the same.

1 May 1746 O. S., Page 30
Upon the Petition of James Gee and others which was referr'd to the Consideration of this Court It appearing that the Road Petitioned for will be in the County of Lunenburg when the dividing Line is run between this County and that Order'd that the said Petition be Rejected.

5 June 1746 O. S., Page 37
Order'd That John Wall Michael Wall and George Hicks Gent or either of them be appointed to acquaint the Court of Isle of Wight County that the Bridge over Maherrin River and Donaldson's wants rebuilding and that they be likewise appointed in conjunction with such persons as shall be nominated by that Court to employ workmen to rebuild the same.

5 June 1746 O. S., Page 38
Order'd That Lewis Parham Gent be appointed to acquaint the Court of Surry County that the Bridge over Nottoway River at Sweeds is greatly out of repair and wants rebuilding And that he be also appointed in conjunction with such Persons as shall be Nominated by that Court to employ Workmen to rebuild the same.

3 July 1746 O. S., Page 40
It appearing that the Road lately cleared from Allen's Mill to Nottoway River near Harrison's Middle Quarter in this County in which John Wall and John Willis Gent were appointed to desire the Court of Surry County to continue from the opposite Side of the said River thro' that County to Sapponey Creek will cross the said River within two or three Miles of a Bridge on the same at Sweed's and that there must of necessity be another Bridge over the said River if the s^d. Road is continued the charge of which will be very burthensome to the Inhabitants of this County Order'd that the said Wall and Willis desist from making application to the Court of Surry County for the purpose aforesaid and that Richard Ransone Surveior of that part of the said Road already cleared be discharged from any farther attendance on the same.

INDEX - BRUNSWICK COUNTY ROAD ORDERS

This index is arranged by subject: Personal Names; Bridges; Chapels, Churches; Ferries and Landings; Fords; Houses; Mills; Geographic Features, etc.; Plantations; Rivers, Creeks, Runs, Swamps, etc.; Quarters; Miscellaneous; Roads

Personal Names

William Acock, 23, 24
John Adcocke, 15
James Adkins, 28
Martha Alexander, 30
David Allen, 24
Robert Allen, 34
Coll Allen, 8, 10^2, 13, 16, 20, 21
James Arnold, 5, 12
John Austin, 31
Richard Austin, 31
William Baughstick, 28
David Bailes, 8, 10, 19
Thomas Bailes, 13
William Barter, 28
John Bartholomew, 13
Henry Bates, 10
John Batt, 28
Mr. Batte, 10
Henry Bedingfield, 5, 6, 9, 10, 27
John Bently, 28
Mason Bishop, 11^2, 16, 20, 34
John Blackstone, 26
Catherine Blaikley, Widow, 31
William Blaikley, 15
Hugh Boston, 28
John Boucher, 24, 33
Philemon Bowers, 31
Charles Brady, 19
Adam Breakenridge, 37
Robert Breakenridge, 37
W[m]. Bressie, 35
George Brewer (Sen[r].), 8, 19
Howell Brewer, 19
John Brewer, 19
Lanier Brewer, 19
Nicholas Brewer, 23
William Brewer, 19

Robert Briggs, 31
Edward Broadnax, 20
John Brooks, 28
Robert Brooks, 34
Abraham Browne, 17, 32
Burwell Brown, 10
Godfrey Brown, 26
Jeremiah Brown, 10
John Browne, 22
Richard Bryan, 13
Thomas Bull, 33
Richard Burch/Burke, 6, 18, 23, 35
M^r. Burch, 20
Thomas Burnett, 8
Lewis Burwell, 37
Thomas Busbey, 8
John Butcher, 6, 7, 18
Thomas Calford, 34
Edward Calwell, 26
John Calwell, 34
Charles Campbell, 31
Cornelius Cargill, 18, 24, 25
John Cargill, 33, 35
Cargill, 9
Daniel Carrel, 32
Nathaniel Carter, 19
Thomas Carter, 10
John Cate, 25
William Cate, 10
Samuel Chamberlain, 7, 8, 15, 17, 18
John Chapman, 8, 21, 29, 30, 32
John Chavas, 34
John Clyburn, 8
John Cole, 23, 24, 34
Major Cole, 37
James Coleman, 20, 25, 27
William Collier, 10, 28
Joseph Colson, 16, 19
Thomas Connoway, 31
Henry Cook, 8, 10, 27
John Cooke, 5, 19, 29
Robert Coock/Cooke, 24, 34
Edward Cordle, 34
Thomas Couch Senr., 19
Thomas Couch ju^r., 19
Willian Couch, 19

Thomas Crawford, 24
Saml Crawley, 5, 11, 12, 20, 22, 24
Matthew Creed, 14, 16, 17, 22
James Cunningham, 37
William Cunningham, 37
Patrick Damm, 19, 21
Stephen Dampier, 26
Hugh Daniel, 32
John Davis, 10, 11
William Davis, 15
John Day, 17, 26
George Dearden, 23, 30
Christopher De Graffenreidt, 31
Edward Denton, 28
Thomas Denton, 28
Charles Dinkins, 25
James Dinkins, 25
William Dishmall, 22
Charles Dodson, 11
William Dodson, 11
Benjamin Chapman Donaldson, 18, 20, 22, 26
Mr. Donaldson, 27
John Douglass, 8, 17, 18, 19
Robert Douglass, 10
William Douglass, 10, 11
John Drue/Dren, 31, 34
James Duke, 5^2
John Duke, 5, 11, 16, 17, 18, 19, 21^2, 23, 29, 30
William Duke, 5
John Dunkley, 30
Moses Dunkley, 25, 33
Joseph Dunman, 12, 27, 30
John Dunn, 13
Lewis Dupre, 10
Robert Dyer/Dier, 5, 31
Robert Henry Dyer, 26
Graves Eaves, 19
William Eaves, 19
Henry Edloe, 20
John Edloe, 20
Howel Edmunds, 30
John Edwards, 5
Nathaniel (Natt, Matt) Edwards, 13, 14, 20^2
William Edwards, 31
Francis Elledge, 29, 32
Jeremy Ellidge, 32

Henry Embry, 6, 9, 11, 16, 17, 18^2, 19, 25, 27, 35
Capt. Embry, 6
John Evans, 5, 25
John Ezell, 10
William Ezel, 28
John Ezwell, 34
Redman Fallon, 36
Hubbert Farrill, 29
John ffennell/Fennel, 10, 26, 31
William Fletcher, 22
Samuel fflowers, 6, 11
Josia Floyd, 34
John Forest, 37
Henry ffox, 7, 8^2, 9, 11
William Fuqua, 29, 31
John Gardiner, 25
James Gee, 37^2, 38
Robert Gee, 14, 37
William Ghent, Gent, 24, 27^2, 32, 33
Edward Giveins, 37
Edward Goodrich, 28
John Godwyn, 28
James Gordle, 14
William Goss, 34^2
William Gower, 5, 23, 28, 30^2
Joseph Gray, 30
Edward Green, 28
Richard Griffin, 37
William Gunn, 23, 25
John Hagood, 22
William Hagood, 5, 12, 22
James Haley, 10
John Hall, 34
James Halsey, 22
William Hampton, 31
George Harper, 28
Arthur Harris, 13, 15, 20
Benjamin Harrison, 20, 26, 28, 36
Maj^r Benjamin Harrison, 29
Coll^o Harrison, 6, 16, 22
Joseph Hart, 24
John Harwell, 5, 29
Samuel Harwell, 10, 13, 15
Richard Hawkins, 32
William Hawkins, 26
Alexander Hayes, 24

Joseph Heathcock, 8, 19
Edward Henlin, 34
John Hewin, 24
Thomas Hewit, 10
Daniel Hicks/Hix, 13, 15
George Hicks/Hix, 18, 21, 22, 24, 25, 29, 38
James Hicks, 34
John Hix, 34
Joseph Hicks, 34
Robert Hicks, 10, 17
Laurance Higgins, 10
John Hilerease, 22
Robert Hill, 10
Henry Hoe, 6
William Hogan, 13, 18, 21
Samuel Holmes, 19
Jonathan Horsford, 34
Samuel Horsford, 4
William Hough, 19
James House, 10
Lawrence House/Hows, 13, 22, 24
Thomas House, 10^2
Thomas House ju^r, 10
Willm. House, 10
Richard Huckabee/Huckaby, 5, 16, 23
William Huff, 26
Humphry Hughy/Hewey, 32, 34
John Hulin, 19
Griffin Humphris, 22
John Humphris, 14, 23
Robert Humphries, 5, 6, 11^2, 14, 18, 21, 35
John Hurt, 28
John Irby, 8
Doctor Irby, 7, 18
Henry Ivey, 28
Ambrose Jackson, 10, 28
Henry Jackson, 34
John Jackson, 8, 9^2, 10, 19, 22
Ralph Jackson, 34
Thomas Jackson, 5, 10, 28, 34
John Jeffers, 19
Charles Jenkins, 10, 33
John Jinkins, 28
William Jenkins, 29
Marmaduke Johnson, 8, 9
William Johnson, 36

Henry Jones, 16, 28
Hix Jones, 16
Lewellin Jones, 16
Richard Jones, 28
Capt. Richard Jones, 22
Thomas Jones, 26^2, 27, 28, 31, 34
William Jones, 6, 16
Mary Jordan, 28
Thomas Jordan, 10
William Jordan, 28, 33
Cornelius Keith, 26, 30
William Kelley, 20
Benjaming Kymball, 12
Charles Kimball, 5^2, 7, 15
Joseph Kimbal, 5
William Kymball/Kimball, 12, 13, 34
Charles King, 9, 24
William King, 28
Samuel Kyrk, 10
Byrd Lanier, 15
Byrd Thomas Lanier, 22
Nicholas Lanier, 14, 20, 24, 35
Thomas Lanier/Lenoir, 15, 30, 31, 32
Thomas Laurence, 13
William Lax, 28
Henry Ledbetter, 13, 14
John Leadbetter/Ledbetter, 8, 10
Richard Ledbetter, 13, 14, 23, 29
Richard Ledbetter Ju^r, 27
Francis Lett, 29
Willian Linch, 8
Thomas Lloyd, 14
James Love, 31
John Lucas, 10
William Lucas, 29
James Lunday, 10
Thomas Lych, 19
Willm. Macadow, 37
John McAvail, 32
Edmond ^{m}. Carthy, 10
James Mackdaniel, M^c. Daniel, 14^2, 22
Thomas Macclehaney, 37
John Maclin, 23
William Macklin/Maclin, 6, 9, 12, 14, 16, 22
George Mabry, 28
Hinckey/Hinchey Mabry, 28, 30

John Maddin, 33
William Madin, 38
Samuel Manning, 27
Charles Matthews, 22, 27, 31
Ezekiel Matthews, 34
Isaac Matthews, 22
James Matthews, 18, 22, 29
James Matthews ju^r, 22
John Matthews, 22
Matthew Matthews, 31
[illegible] Matthews, 31
Joseph Mayes, 37
Mattox Mayes, 37
Edward Meacham, 28
John Mead, 37
William Melton, 13
John Meritt, 11, 12
Merridith, 28
William Middleton, 34
John Mitchell, 33
Ninian Mitchell, 19
Peter Mitchell, 21
Robert Mitchell, 37
James Mize, 24
Jerimiah Mize, 7
Jonathan Moate, 26
William Mobley, 28
John Moore, 34
William Moore, 29
Henry Morriss, 7, 16^2, 25, 32, 33, 34
Josep Moreton, 34
Andrew Moreman, 34
John Moseley, 19
William Moseley, 19, 23
Robert Munford, 16
Daniel Murfey, 34
Daniel Nantz, 15, 34
David Nantz, 34
Julius Nicholous, 37
James Nipper, 34
John Naper/Nipper, 11, 34, 36
John Nipper Ju^r, 24
Thomas Nunn, 31
James Oliver, 14, 17
Robert Page, 13
James Parham, 8

Lewis Parham, 24, 38
Matthew Parham, 10
Joseph Parks, 10, 28
William Parks, 10
Richard Parr, 22
Charles Parrish, 26, 31
James Parrish, 16, 34, 38
John Parsons, 30
Thomas Parsons, 10, 20, 21, 29
Edward Pennington, 30
John Peoples, 28
Nathaniel Perry, 10[3]
Thomas Person, 31
Batte Petterson/Peterson, 10, 18, 21[2], 23[2], 31
John Peterson, 30
John Pettway, 28
John Platt, 34
William Pool, 5
Seth Petty Poole, 30, 37
Belian Possey, 28
Douglass Powell, 19
John Powell, 19
Thomas Powell, 19
Thomas Powell ju^r, 19
William Powell, 19
Capt. Poytris, 8
Richard Ramsey, 11
Josias Randle, 12, 24, 31, 32, 35
Col^o. Richard Randolph, 33, 34
Richard Ransone, 38
Clement Read, 11[2], 14, 15, 20
Evan Rease/Rees, 28, 34
ffoster Reaves, 10
Thomas Reaves, 10
Thomas Reaves ju^r., 10
Timothy Reaves, 10
William Reaves, 11, 12, 22
Robert Renard/Reynard, 5, 28
William Reynolds, 22
James Rigsby, 11, 12, 22, 35
William Rivers, 26, 31
William Roark, 19
John Roberts, 24
Phillip Roberts, 34
Edward Robinson, 34
George Robinson, 32

John Rook, 19
John Rose, 5, 17
William Rose, 21
John Ross, 7
Henry Rottenbury, 12, 34
Richard Rottenbury, 34
Samuel Russell, 28
Thomas Sadler, 33
Robert Sanford, 20, 22
Thomas Sandford, 25
James Saxon, 8
Lizwell Saxon, 8
Paul Sears, 13
John Seering, 5
John Shearing, 28
Joseph Shearing, 28
Adam Sims, 9
William Sims, 10
Henry Simmons, 16
Peter Simmons, 28
David Sinclair, 34
William Sinkfield, 10
Stephen Sissons, 28
William Sissons, 28
Patrick Smith, 13
Richard Smith, 5, 11, 19, 22, 23
Roger Smith, 13
William Smith, 5, 9^2, 10, 11, 28
William Smith Junr., 10
Mr Smith, 31
Alex^r. Southerland, 28
Robert Southerland, 28, 33
William Southerland, 28
Thomas Spell, 34
ffrancis Steed, 8
John Steed, 32, 36
Thomas Stephens, 23
Charles Stewart, 22, 24, 25
Drury Stith, 19, 25
John Stoell, 12
William Stroud, 18, 24
Michael Sullivant, 10
Mary Syms, 8
Edward Swanson, 22, 29
Richard Swansome/Swanson, 5, 22
Matthew Talbott, 28, 34

Richard Taliaferro, 36
Anthony Tann, 34
Hosea Tapley, 9^3, 15, 16
China Tatum, 34
Edward Tatum, 5, 7^2
Joseph Tatum, 34
Peter Tatum, 34
Henry Taylor, 31
John Thomson, 12
George Tillman, 29
Roger Tillman, 12, 13, 29
Amos Timms, 33
Toby, 26
John Tomerlin, 10
Widdow trap, 10
Francis Troublefeild, 34
John Tuke, 28
James Turner, 19
Simon Turner, 10
John Twitty, 28, 34, 37
James Upchurch, 23
William Upchurch, 23
Charles Valentine, 31
William Vaughan, 9
Thomas Venton, 10
Thos. Vernon, 37
John Walker, 8
John Wall, 7, 8^2, 9, 11^3, 16, 17, 18^3, 19, 20, 21^3, 23^2, 25^2, 27, 30, 31, 35, 38^2
Michael Wall, 10, 12, 22, 24, 30, 31, 35, 36^2, 38
William Wall, 7
William Walters, 12
George Walton, 6, 7, 8, 35
Joseph Warberton, 5
Warwick, 26
James Watson, 10
Edward Wearham, 10
Richard Weatherford, 8
William White, 37
William Whittamore, 9^2
John Williams, 13
Lazarus Williams, 26^2
Richard Williams, 26
William Williamson, 28
John Willis, 38
Saml: Willson, 37
Thomas Wilson, 5, 10, 15, 23

Thomas Winford, 28, 31
John Winningham, 33
Benjamin Winsley, 37
John Wise, 19
William Wise Senr., 19
William Wise ju^r, 19
Richard Woods, 34
James Wortham, 29
Benjamin Wray, 10
ffrancis Wray, 12, 20, 23^2
John Wray, 23, 28
Francis Renn (Wrenn), 13
Joseph Wrenn, 10
Wil^m.Wrenn, 10
Henry Wych, 8^2, 18
Peter Wych, 28
William Wynne, 9, 16, 28
ffrancis Wyrick, 10
John Wyrick, 11
Joseph [missing], 5
Patrick [missing], 15
Ralph [missing], 5
Thomas [illegible] ssum, 28

Bridges

Allen's Creek Bridge, 32
Byrd's Quarter Bridge (Maherrin), 35
Cooks Creek bridge, 24
Cut Bank Bridge, 28
lower Cut bank Bridge, 29
upper Cut Banks Bridge (Maherrin), 13
Upper Cut Bank Bridge (Nottoway), 35
Lower cut banks bridge (Nottoway), 7, 8, 12, 13, 14, 15, 20, 27, 35
Cosway to Lower cut banks bridge (Nottoway), 13
bridge near Benjamin Chapman Donaldson's (Maherrin), 18, 20, 27, 28, 29, 30, 31, 35, 38
bridge below the mouth of Fountain's Creek (Maherrin), 33
Great Creek bridge, 22
Hix's Ford Bridge (Maherrin), 35
Little Creek bridge, 10
Mize's Ford Bridge, 38
Otterdam Bridge, 24
Shining Creek bridge, 22
Sweades bridge (Nottoway), 16, 17, 18, 21, 22, 24, 25, 30, 32, 35
three Creeks bridge, 21^2, 22^2, 23^2

Waqua Creek Bridge, 36

Chapels, Churches

Chappel, 5
Church, 5, 7, 9, 14, 26, 30
Roanoke Chappel, 24

Ferries and Landings

Alexander's Landing, 26
Cornelius Keith's ferry at Horse ford on Roanoke River, 26
Cornelius Keiths Landing, 30
ferry at Hiks's Ford, 17
Horse Foard ferry, 29, 36
Taylor's Landing, 31

Fords

Foard on Bannister river, 35^2
ford a little below Butchers on Roanoke, 7
Cargills Foard (Staunton River), 35^2
Chamberlain's Ford, 8^2, 10, 17^2
Hicks's Ford, 8, 12, 17, 35
Capt. Hicks's Ford, 24
William Hogan's ford (north fork Roanoke), 13
Horse fford (Roanoke), 5, 26, 29
Island ford, 16
Jones ffoard, 6, 16
Joseph Mayes's New Ford (Staunton), 37
Robert Mitchell's Ford, 37
Mize's Ford, 38
ford near Munford's Plantation (Stanton), 21
North Ford, 20
Peterson's Ford (ffountain's Creek), 28
ford where its common to ride over on Roan oak Road (Maherrin), 33
Adam Sim's ford, 9
Roger Smith's fford, 13
Smith's Ford, 20
Sweeds/Sweades ford (Nottoway), 9, 16, 17, 18, 19
Western ford (Maherrin), 14
old Westward ford (Maherrin), 13, 15
Henry Wych's fford (Maherrin), 8

Houses

Cook's House on Hounds Creek, 26[2]
William Macklin's House, 6, 16

Mills

Col. Allens Mill, 13, 21, 38
Benjamin Harrison's Mill, 28
Maj[r] Benjamin Harrison's Mill, 29
Jacksons Mill, 7[2], 8
Thomas Jones's Mill, 27
Drury Stith's Mill, 19
John Wall's Mill, 8

Geographic Features, etc.

Chunketapusso, 8, 16, 25
Coals's old Field, 29
Colledge (of William & Mary), 28
Lower Cut banks, 24, 25
upper Cut Banks (Maherrin River), 6, 13
Duke's Race Paths, 28, 29
the fort (at Christanna), 6, 9, 10, 12[2], 14
Thomas Jones's fish Dam, 28
Long Mountain, 38
Main Ridge between Maherrin & Roanoke, 5, 6, 9
Ridge between Appomattox and Roanoke Rivers, 29
Fork of Roan oak, 24, 32
Wolf Pit at Coleman's Path, 19
Douglass's Wolf Pit, 9

Plantations

Coll Allens Plantation, 10
Embry's Plantation, 28
John Hall's Plantation, 34
Howses Plantation, 10
Thomas Jones's Plantation, 28
Mize's Plantation, 14
Munford's Plantation, 16, 21

Powel's Plantation, 16
Capt Poytris's Plantation on ffountain's Creek, 8
Talbotts Plantation, 28
Richard Taliaferro's Plantation, 36
Walker's Plantation, 16
Michael Wall's Plantation, 10
Walters's Plantation, 19
Richard Woods Plantation, 34

Rivers, Creeks, Runs, Swamps, etc.

Aaron's Creek, 36
Allen's Creek, 18, 32^2,
Appomattox River, 29, 37
Bannister river, 35
Beaver pond Creek, 19
Buckshorn/Buckhorn Creek, 18, 19
Butcher's Creek, 7^2, 18, 37
Cane branch, 8
Coldwater Run, 8
Cooks/Cockes Creek, 24, 34, 36
Cubb Creek, 29, 37
Fall Creek, 36
Falling River, 37
Flatt Creek, 34
Flat Rock/flatt Rock Creek, 12, 20^2, 37
ffountains/Fountains Creek, 8, 10, 28, 33, 36
Great Creek, 8, 9, 13, 14, 16, 22, 26
G [missing] Swamp, 8
Haw Tree Creek, 5
Hickory Run, 6
Honey Hill run, 9
Hounds Creek, 26
Jack Swamp, 33
Jeneto Creek, 36
Jackson's Mill Swamp, 8
Ledbetters Creek, 33
Little Creek, 10
Lizard Creek, 19
Long Branch, 18, 19
Maherrin River, 5^2, 6^2, 8, 9^2, 12, 13^3, 14^2, 17^3, 18, 19^3, 20, 22, 24^2, 26, 27, 30, 31, 32, 33, 34, 35^2, 37^2, 38^2
Miles's Creek, 18
Nottoway River, 5, 6^2, 7, 8, 9, 11^3, 12, 13, 14, 16, 17, 18^2, 19, 20^2, 21, 22, 23, 24, 26^2, 27^2, 28, 31^2, 32, 33, 35^3, 38^2

great Nottoway River, 31
Poplar Spring, 37
Quarrel Swamp, 13
Rattle Snake Swamp/Creek, 14, 19, 20
Reads Creek, 28
Reaves's Swamp, 29
Reedy Creek, 5^2, 7^2, 9, 12, 16^2, 17, 19, 24, 25, 34
Roanoke/Roenoke River, 5^3, 6, 7^3, 11, 13, 15, 18^2, 24, 26, 29, 30, 32
first great Creek of Roenoke River, 5
little Roanoke River (Roanoke Creek), 28, 33
Rockey Creek, 6, 7
Sapponey Creek, 38
Shining Creek, 15, 22
Stanton/Staunton River, 21, 35^2
Stith's Creek, 5, 6, 7
Sturgeon Runn, 6, 11, 12, 14, 16, 18, 23
Taylor's Creek, 6
three Creeks, 9, 21^2, 22^2, 23^2
Turnip Creek, 29, 37
Waqua Creek, 11^3, 16, 27, 30, 31, 32, 36
Wild Catt Creek, 22

Quarters

Coll Allens Quarter, 10, 13
Col^l. Byrd's quarter at Maherrin, 24, 35
Mr. Battes Quarter, 10
Christopher DeGraffenreidt's Quarter, 31
Fisher's Quarter, 31
Coll^o Harrisons Quarters, 6, 9, 14
Harrison's Quarter Called Sweeds, 10
Harrison's Middle Quarter, 38
Munford's Quarter, 6, 7
Col^o. Richard Randolphs Quarter at the mouth of Little Roan oak, 33
Tabbs Quarter on Waqua, 30

Miscellaneous

Amelia County Court, 33
Amelia Court House, 27
Brunswick County Line, 5, 8, 10, 12, 19
old Brunswick County Line, 9^2, 16
Brunswick County Court House, 5, 7, 14^2, 17, 28, 30, 32
the Country line (not to be confused with the County line; this is the Virginia line), 32, 36

General Court (at Williamsburg), 9
Isle of Wight County, 18, 20, 29[2], 30, 31, 38
Isle of Wight County Court, 18, 20, 29[2], 30, 31, 37
Lunenburg County, 38
Prince George County, 6, 7, 8, 9, 25, 27, 35[2]
Prince George County Court, 6, 7, 8, 9, 25, 27, 35[2]
Signposts and Direction Stones, 26
Charles Stewart's Shop, 24
Surry County, 7, 11, 16, 17, 18, 19, 20, 21, 32, 38[2]
Surry County Court, 11, 16, 17, 18, 19, 20, 21, 32, 38[2]

Roads

Road from Aaron's Creek to Robert Mitchell's Ford, 37

Amelia Road, 31

Road from Waqua at Briggs's to the Amelia Road at Nottoway River, 31

Amelia Court House Road, 27

Road from Waqua to Nottoway River to meet the Road from Amelia Court House as the Path now goes by Thomas Jones's Mill, 27

Road from the head of Appomattox to Poplar Spring against the North end the Long Mountain, 37

Road from near the mouth of Turnip Creek to the Ridge between Appomattox and Roan oak Rivers, 29

Bedingfields Road, 7, 8

road from Chunketapusso to Bedingfield's Road, 8

road from a ford on Roanoke a little below Butchers into Bedingfield's Road, 7

Briggs's Road, 31

Burch's Road, 11, 31

M[r]. Burch's Road, 20[2], 22

Road from flatt Rock Creek by Mason Bishop's into M[r]. Burch's Road, 20 bridle path from Richard Woods Plantation into the Road by Mason Bishops, 34

Road from Burch's Road to Briggs's Road, 31

Road from Wild Catt into Burch's Road, 22

Road from Miles's Creek to John Butcher's, 18

Butcher's Road, 16, 24, 32, 34

Road from the bridge at Cooks Creek to Butcher's Road, 24

Road from Cocks Creek to Butchers Road, 34

Road from the Island ford to Butcher's Road, 16

Cargill's Road, 21

Road from Chamberlains fford into the Old Road at the Little Creek bridge thence along the old Road Round Coll Allens Plantation between Allens and Howses, 10

Briddle Way from Chamberlains ford to Jackson's Mill Swamp where Tatum's Road Crosses it, 8

Briddle Road from John Wall's Mill to Chamberlain's Ford, 8

Chamberlain's Road, 13

Road from Roger Smith's fford up to Chamberlain's Road, 13

Church Road, 11, 14, 16, 19

Church Road from the great Creek, 14, 26

Church Road from Harrison's Quarter on the Great Creek to the Church, 9

Road from Robert Humphris's to the Church, 14

bridle way from William Maclin's House into the Church Road, 16

Road from Maherrin River to the Church, 5

Road from Smith's Ford to the Church Road, 20

Road from Waqua into the Church Road, 11

bridleway from Tabbs Quarter on Waqua to the Church, 30

Cocke's Road, 37

Road from the North Fork of Maherrin River into Cocke's Road, 37

Coleman's Path, 19

Road to the Wolf Pit at Coleman's Path, 19

Henry Cook's Road, 10, 27

Road from opposite to Nathaniel Perry's into Henry Cooks Road Near Michael Wall's Plantation where the Widdow trap lives, 10

Road from the County Lyne by Thomas Jordan's to Nathaniel Perry's, 10

Cooke's Road, 36

Major Cole's Road, 37

Court Road, 19

Road from Drury Stith's Mill into the Court Road, 19

Court House Road, 16, 28

Road from Benjamin Harrison's Mill to the Court House Road to the Cut Bank Bridge, 28

bridleway from Nicholas Lanier's house to the Court House, 14

road from Court House to Sturgeon Run, 14

Road from Brunswick Courthouse to Surry, 7

Road from the Waqua to the Courthouse, 32

Road from John Duke's Race Paths to the lower Cut bank Bridge, 29

Lower Cut Bank Road, 33

Road that leads from Henry Cook's Road to the Bridge that leads over Maherrin River at Mr. Donaldson's, 27

Road from Peterson's Ford on ffountains Creek to Donaldson's Bridge, 28

Edwards's Path, 34

Road from Reedy Creek to Edwards's Path, 34

Road from Fall Creek to the Country Line, 36

old fort road, 28

Road that leads from the fort over the Lower Cutbanks of Nottoway, 14

Road from Jack Swamp to the bridge that is building below the mouth of Fountains Creek, 33

Governours Road, 17[2]

Road from Chamberlains ford over Maherrin to the Governours Road, 17

road from Hicks Ford to the County Line, 8, 12

Hix's Road, 22

Road from Horse Ford Ferry to Cock's Creek and to Jeneto, 36

Road from the Horse fford over Roenoke River to the Ridge between Roenoke and Maherrin River, 5

Humphris's Church Path, 16

Road leading from Humphris's Church Path to the great Creek near Mason Bishop's, 16

Isle of Wright Road, 29

Road from Maj^r Benjamin Harrison's Mill over Reaves's Swamp to meet the Isle of Wight Road, 29

Road from the County line near the lizard Creek down to the Road on Rattle Snake, 19

Henry Ledbetters old path, 13

Road from the North Fork of Maherrin River to the Head of Butcher's Creek, 37

Road from Col^l. Byrd's quarter at Maherrin to Roan oake Chappel, 24

Road from Flatt Creek to Maherrin River, 34

Road from Maherrin River above William Macklins House, 6

Road on the North Side of Maherrin from Capt. Hicks's Ford to Charles Stewart's Shop, 24

Road from Maherrin River near Walters's to the Long Branch, 19

Road from the North Ford on Rattle Snake Swamp to the Western ford of Maherrin to Rattlesnake, 20

road from Richard Ledbetter's on Rattle Snake Swamp to the Western ford on Maherrin and over ye River into the Road that leads from the fort over the Lower Cut banks of Nottoway, 14

Road from Capp^t Poytris's Plantation on ffountains Creek to Henry Wych's fford over Meherrin, 8

Road from the Main Road near Robinson's on Maherrin and on the Ridge as Young's goes to the Country line, 4

Maherrin Road, 13

old Road from Allens Mill to the Maherrin Road, 13

old Maherrin Road, 25

Main Road, 14, 32

road from Maherrin River near Mizes to the Main Road, 14

Road from Meherrin River to the Otter Dams (over three Creeks Bridge), 21

Nottoway Road, 15

Road from Nottoway Road to Shining Creek, 15

Road from a Blaz'd White Oake on the Ridge between Nottoway & Maherrin Rivers between Thomas Jones & Toby's to Cook's House on Hounds Creek, 26

Road from Nottoway River to the Chappel, 5

Road from Cook's House on Hounds Creek to Nottoway River Below the Fork, 26

Road from Christopher DeGraffenreidt's Quarter to great Nottoway River a little above Fisher's Quarter, 31

Old Road, 10

Road from Nottoway River at Thomas Jones's fish Dam to the old Road Near Duke's Race Paths, 28

King's High Way from Nottoway River to Sturgeon Runn, 6, 18

Road from Nottoway River near Richard Burkes to Sturgeon Run, 28

Road from Robert Humphris's into Burch's Road along the Ridge between Sturgeon Run and Waqua, 11

Road from Nottoway River to Waqua, 11

Road from Jones Ford over Waqua into the Court House Road between Sturgeon Runn & Waqua, 16

Road from the old Brunswick Line to the Reedy Creek, 5, 9, 16

Road from Chunketapusso to the Reedy Creek, 16, 25

Road that leads from the Court House to the Reedy Creek, 5, 17

Road from the Reedy Creek to Maherrin, 19

Road from Reedy Creek below Jackson's Mill into the Road that leads from this Courthouse to Surry County, 7

Road from Reedy Creek below Jackson's Mill to the Church, 7

Road from the Ready Creek to the Lower Cut banks, 24

Road from the branches of Reedy Creek to the Road that is cleared to Flatt Rock, 37

Road from the Flatt Rock of the Reedy Creek to Christiana ffort, 12

Roan oak/Roenoke/Roanoake Road, 10, 33

Roanoak Road from the Ridge out, 15, 23

Road from the fort to the Roanoake Road, 10

Road from Allen's Creek to the fork of Roanoak, 32

Road from William Hogan's ford over the North fork of Roanoke to [missing] ford on Maherrin River, 13

Road from Roanoke River Near Wm. Hogans to the Long Branch, 18

upper part of the Road from James Mize's to the fork of Roan oak, 24

briddle Road from Jerimiah Mizes to Munfords Quarter up Roanoke, 7

Road from the Ridge between Roanoke and Meherrin, to Maherrin River and from the fort to the other Road above where Carghill lived, 9

Road from Col^o. Richard Randolphs Quarter at the mouth of Little Roan oak til it meets the Road Order'd to be clear'd by Amelia County Court to the Ridge that divides this County from that, 33

Road from Talbotts Plantation on little Roanoak to the Road between Embry's & Thomas Jones's Plantation on the Nap of Reads Creek, 28

Road from Rockey Creek to Jones ffoard, 6

Road from Cargills Foard on Staunton River to a Ford on Bannister River, 35^2

Road from William Hogan's to the Ford over Stanton River near Munford's Plantation into Cargill's Road, 21

Road from Joseph Mayes's New Ford on Stanton River to Turnip Creek below W^m. Cunningham's crossing the said Creek to Cubb Creek at Thos. Vernons and thence crossing Cubb Creek as the old Road runs into Major Cole's Road, 37

Road from the old Brunswick Line to Sweeds ford on Nottoway, 9

Road from Sweed's towards the Courthouse, 30

Road from Thomas Houses to Harrison's Quarter Called Sweeds, 10

Road from Sweeds Bridge into the old Maherrin Road, 25

Tatums's Road, 8, 13

The Trading Path, 4

old trading path, 12

Road from the old trading path to the Road by Benjaming Kymball's, 12

Twitty's Road, 33

Road from Twitty's Road a little below the mouth of Ledbetters creek to Nottoway River, 33

upper Road, 7

Mr.Walls Road, 19

road from Mr.Walls Road about a half a mile from the River to the Beaver pond Creek, 19

briddle way from Quarrel Swamp at Henry Ledbetters old path to the old Westward ford on Maherrin River, 13

west ward path, 7, 15

Road from the west ward path down to Doctor Irby's, 7

old Westward Path, 18

Road from the Westward ford to the old Westward Path, 18

Westward Road, 28

Road from the old fort Road into the Westward Road, 28

Wilsons and Bedingfield's Road, 6

Road from Munford's Quarter up Roenoke into Wilsons and Bedingfields Road, 6

Young's Road, 32

www.ingramcontent.com/pod-product-compliance
Lightning Source LLC
Chambersburg PA
CBHW080554170426
43195CB00016B/2786